ENGLISH LOVE POEMS

ENGLISH LOVE POEMS

*Edited by
John Betjeman and
Geoffrey Taylor*

faber and faber
LONDON · BOSTON

First published in 1957
by Faber and Faber Limited
3 Queen Square London WCIN 3AU
First published in this edition 1964
Reprinted five times
Reissued 1988

Printed in England by
Clays Ltd, St Ives plc

A CIP record for this book is
available from the British Library

ISBN 0 571 07065 5

8 10 9

14=70

CONTENTS

INTRODUCTION

This Anthology has been compiled by two married men in their middle years. Each thinks he knows the joys of love fulfilled and the sorrows of love unrequited. Each believes that poetry, like no other art, can crystallize by using the right words in the right order those thoughts and emotions which love provokes. Most people turn to poetry when they are in love, seeking to find there a definition of what they themselves cannot express in words. We have therefore tried to make this Anthology representative of the different moods of love, rather than representative of our best poets when they write about love. We have not included in our definition of love poetry poems expressing the love of man for God, nor have we included impassioned expressions of the lusts of the flesh.

Our method of selection has been to re-read the poetical works of various poets and the only anthologies we have consulted have been the Elizabethan Song Books and Chambers' and Sidgwick's *Early English Lyrics*. The temptation to read modern anthologies, notably that compiled by John Hayward which we have been told is particularly good, has been avoided. When we have found a love poem we have thought worthy of inclusion, we have typed it out slowly. The process of copying the poem out is in itself a test. Then we have read it out loud. Many more poems were copied out and read than have been included. The process surprised us in showing how disappointing the love poems of some of our best poets were, while the·reading of poetical works showed us that certain great poets like Coleridge and Arnold hardly wrote any love poems at all. When we had copied out 'Come down, O Maid, from yonder mountain height' and read it aloud, we wondered what the girl was doing on the mountain anyway, and decided that the poem was an astonishing piece of virtuosity, not a love poem. We found Tennyson's beautiful tribute to his wife when he was seventy-seven (page

124) a more touching and genuine expression of love. In our testing other poets we had expected to include, failed us. Swinburne's erotic poetry which seemed so marvellous to us when we were younger, seems to us in middle age not love but adolescent imagination. Shelley, who is generally regarded as *the* poet of love, seemed meaningless froth, and even Byron did not compare as a love poet with Tom Moore.

We are asked to make an anthology of English love poems, and because of this, conspicuously Celtic poems have been omitted as not being in the English mood. Moore is not an exception for his love poems are in the English mood and idiom. The greatest love poet in these islands was, we think, Robert Burns, but his best love poems are almost always in Scottish dialect and if we were to admit Scottish dialect poems and beautiful Irish love poems, such as 'The Outlaw of Logh Legne' and 'O woman stately as the swan', this anthology would have been twice its size and not what our publishers required. No American poets have been included.

We have not been equally responsible for choosing the poems in various periods. For instance, one of us is comparatively better read in the poets of the seventeenth century and the other knows more about the nineteenth. Only one of us has chosen the poems written since the first war. If this had not been agreed to, the other would not have allowed any of his poems to be included.

J.B.
G.T.

GEOFFREY TAYLOR

In November 1955 Geoffrey Taylor wrote to me about this
anthology we were to do together, 'I want to do it my own way—
the long way, of reading the poets without consulting existing
anthologies—my view being that there are probably as good fish
in the forest as ever got into an anthology. The easy way would
be to go through the various "Oxford Books" (I have them all),
copy out the famous bits and have the whole thing done by Xmas
—no fun for anyone. As it is, by about March we'll have something
good and fairly original anyway; and I, at least, will have read so
much Love that I'll probably never love again.' Geoffrey died at his
house in Dublin eight months later, having completed this antho-
logy and done all the hard work for it. One of his last conscious
acts was to approve the preface which appears over our joint
initials.

Geoffrey Taylor was born on 5th April 1900 at Wroxham,
Norfolk, the eldest son of Basil Phibbs of Lisheen, County Sligo,
and Rebekah Wilbraham Taylor of Hall Place, Hertfordshire.
When he was grown up, he took his mother's name. He went to
Haileybury in 1914 and in 1918 joined the Royal Irish Rifles, but
the war ended before he had finished his training in Belfast. For a
very short time he was at Trinity College, Dublin, and then studied
under Professor Carpenter at the Royal College of Science. He was
always a keen botanist and gardener, and wrote a standard work
on the Victorian Flower Garden. His other interest was poetry
ancient and modern. At one time he had a printing press at Sutton
Veny in England, and it was there that Sir William Nicholson
painted the well-known portrait of him. Geoffrey never lost the
look of youth seen in that portrait, the fierce expression, the long
lock of hair and the burning fervour in his dark eyes. He was the
kindest and most self-disciplined man I ever knew. He encouraged

the unconfident and discovered new poets. Indeed, it was one of his chief delights to unearth unrecognized talent. His editorship of *The Bell* (the Irish equivalent of *Horizon*) will long be remembered. Geoffrey always retained his integrity and, such were his humour, sense of proportion, goodness and force of character, that he kept out of all literary disputes in London and Dublin. He was twice married, first to Norah McGuinness and then to Mary Dillwyn who survives him with a daughter and son.

He was a considerable poet and besides publications of his own poetry, he edited anthologies and wrote a travel book on Ireland. His large library was mostly of poetry and he never allowed space in it for any poet who did not come up to his own high standards. He took endless trouble, in a vast correspondence, over the work of aspiring and unestablished poets.

JOHN BETJEMAN

QUI BIEN AIME A TARD OUBLIE

Now welcom somer, with thy sonne softe,
That hast wintres weders over-shake,
And driven awey the longe nightes blake!

Seynt Valentyn, that art ful hy on lofte,
Thus singen smale foules for thy sake
  'Now welcom somer, with thy sonne softe,
  That hast this wintres weders over-shake.'

Wel han they cause for to gladen ofte,
Sith ech of hem recovered hath his make;
Ful blisful may they singen whan they wake;
  'Now welcom somer, with thy sonne softe,
  That hast this wintres weders over-shake,
  And driven awey the longe nightes blake.'

MERCILES BEAUTE

Your yèn two wol slee me sodenly,
I may the beautè of hem not sustene,
So woundeth hit through-out my herte kene.

And but your word wol helen hastily
My hertes wounde, whyl that hit is grene,
  Your yèn two wol slee me sodenly,
  I may the beautè of hem not sustene.

Upon my trouthe I sey yow feithfully,
That ye ben of my lyf and deeth the quene;
For with my deeth the trouthe shal be sene.
  Your yèn two wol slee me sodenly,
  I may the beautè of hem not sustene,
  So woundeth hit through-out my herte kene.

*

So hath your beautè fro your hertè chaced
Pitee, that me ne availeth not to pleyne;
For Daunger halt your mercy in his cheyne.

Giltles my deeth thus han ye me purchaced;
I sey yow sooth, me nedeth not to feyne;
  So hath your beautè fro your hertè chaced
  Pitee, that me ne availeth not to pleyne.

Allas! that nature hath in yow compassed
So greet beautè, that no man may atteyne
To mercy, though he sterve for the peyne.
So hath your beautè fro your hertè chaced
  Pitee, that me ne availeth not to pleyne;
  For Daunger halt your mercy in his cheyne.

*

Sin I fro Love escapèd am so fat,
I never thenk to ben in his prison lene;
Sin I am free, I counte him not a bene.

He may answere, and seye this or that;
I do no fors, I speke right as I mene.
  Sin I fro Love escapèd am so fat,
  I never thenk to ben in his prison lene.

Love hath my name y-strike out of his sclat,
And he is strike out of my bokes clene
For ever-mo; ther is non other mene.
  Sin I fro Love escapèd am so fat,
  I never thenk to ben in his prison lene;
  Sin I am free, I counte him not a bene.

My Gostly fader, I me confesse,
   First to God and then to you,

   That at a window—wot ye how?—
I stale a cosse of grete sweteness,
Which don was out aviséness;
   But hit is doon not undoon now.
My gostly fader, I me confesse,
   First to God and then to you.

But I restore it shall doubtless
   Agein, if so be that I mow;
   And that to God I make a vow
And elles I axé foryefness.
My gostly fader, I me confesse,
   First to God and then to you.

Alas, that ever that speche was spoken
   That the fals aungel seid to me!
Alas! oure maker's bidding is broken,
   For I have touched his owen dere tree.
Oure flescly eyn bin all unloken;
   Naked for sinne oureself we see;
That sory appel that we ham soken
   To dethe hathe brouth my spouse and me.

What meanest thou, my fortune,
   From me so fast to fly?
Alas, thou art importune
   To work thus cruelly.

Thy waste continually
   Shall cause me call and cry;
Woe worth the time that I
   To love did first apply.

*

Is it not sure a deadly pain,
   To you I say that lovers be,
When faithful hearts must needs refrain
   The one the other for to see?
   I you assure ye may trust me,
Of all the pains that ever I knew,
It is a pain that most I rue.

*

O waly, waly up the bank,
   And waly, waly down the brae,
And waly, waly yon burn-side,
   Where I and my love wont to gae.
I lean'd my back unto an aik,
   I thought it was a trusty tree,
But first it bow'd and syne it brak,
   Sae my true love did lightly me.

O waly, waly, gin love be bonny,
    A little time while it is new,
But when 'tis auld it waxeth cauld,
    And fades away like the morning dew:
O wherefore shou'd I busk my heid?
    Or wherefore shou'd I kame my hair?
For my true love has me forsook,
    And says he'll never love me mair.

Now Arthur-Seat shall be my bed,
    The sheets shall ne'er be 'filed by me,
Saint Anton's well shall be my drink,
    Since my true love has forsaken me.
Martinmas wind, when wilt thou blaw,
    And shake the green leaves off the tree?
O gentle death, when wilt thou come?
    For of my life I am wearie.

Tis not the frost that freezes fell,
    Nor blawing snaw's inclemencie;
Tis not sic cauld that makes me cry,
    But my love's heart grown cauld to me.
When we came in by Glasgow town,
    We were a comely sight to see;
My love was clad in black velvet,
    And I my self in cramasie.

But had I wist before I kiss'd,
    That love had been so ill to win,
I had lockt my heart in a case of gold,
    And pinn'd it with a silver pin.
And, oh! if my young babe were born,
    And set upon the nurse's knee,
And I myself were dead and gone,
    For a maid again I'll never be.

Who shall have my fair lady?
Who shall have my fair lady?
Who but I, who but I, who but I?
  Under the leaves green!

The fairest man
That best love can,
Dandirly, dandirly, dandirly dan,
  Under the leaves green!

*

Western wind, when wilt thou blow,
  The small rain down can rain?
Christ, if my love were in my arms
  And I in my bed again!

JOHN SKELTON
1460–1529

TO MISTRESS MARGARET HUSSEY

Merry Margaret,
  As midsummer flower,
Gentle as falcon
  Or hawk of the tower:
With solace and gladness,
Much mirth and no madness,
All good and no badness;
  So joyously,
  So maidenly,
  So womanly

Her demeaning
In every thing,
Far, far passing
That I can indite,
Or suffice to write
Of Merry Margaret
As midsummer flower,
Gentle as falcon
Or hawk of the tower
And patient and still
And as full of good will
As fair Isaphill,
Coliander
Sweet pomander,
Good Cassander,
Steadfast of thought,
Well made, well wrought,
Far may be sought
Ere that he can find
So courteous, so kind
As Merry Margaret,
This midsummer flower
Gentle as falcon
Or hawk of the tower.

TO MISTRESS MARGERY WENTWORTH

With margerain gentle,
The flower of goodlihead,
Embroidered the mantle
Is of your maidenhead.
Plainly I cannot glose;
Ye be, as I devine,
The pretty primrose,
The goodly columbine.
With margerain gentle,

The flower of goodlihead,
Embroidered the mantle
    Is of your maidenhead.
Benign, courteous, and meek,
    With wordes well devised;
In you, who list to seek,
    Be virtues well comprised.
With margerain gentle,
    The flower of goodlihead,
Embroidered the mantle
    Is of your maidenhead.

SIR THOMAS WYATT
1503–1542

Madame, withouten many words,
    Once, I am sure, ye will or no:
And if ye will, then leave your bourds
    And use your wit, and show it so;

And with a beck ye shall me call.
    And if of one that burneth alway
Ye have any pity at all,
    Answer him fair with yea or nay.

If it be yea, I shall be fain;
    If it be nay, friends as before;
Ye shall another man obtain,
    And I mine own and yours no more.

*

I abide and abide and better abide
(And after the old proverb) the happy day;
And ever my lady to me doth say
'Let me alone and I will provide'.
I abide and abide and tarry the tide,
And with abiding speed well ye may!
Thus do I abide I wot alway
Not her obtaining nor yet denied.
Aye me! this long abiding
Seemeth to me as who sayeth
A prolonging of a dying death
Or a refusing of a desired thing.
Much were it better for to be plain
Than to say 'abide' and yet not obtain.

*

What rage is this? what furour of what kind?
What power, what plague doth weary thus my mind?
Within my bones to rankle is assigned
   What poison, pleasant sweet?

Lo, see, mine eyes swell with continual tears;
The body still away sleepless it wears;
My food nothing my fainting strength repairs,
   Nor doth my limbs sustain.

In deep wide wound the deadly stroke doth turn
To cured scar that never shall return.
Go to, triumph, rejoice thy goodly turn,
   Thy friend thou dost oppress.

Oppress thou dost, and hast of him no cure;
Nor yet my plaint no pity can procure,
Fierce tiger fell, hard rock without recure,
   Cruel rebel to love!

Once may thou love, never beloved again;
So love thou still and not thy love obtain;
So wrathful love with spites of just disdain
   May fret thy cruel heart!

They flee from me that sometime did me seek,
  With naked foot stalking in my chamber.
I have seen them gentle, tame and meek,
  That now are wild and do not remember
  That sometime they put themselves in danger
    To take bread at my hand; and now they range
    Busily seeking with a continual change.

Thankt be fortune, it hath been otherwise
  Twenty times better; but once, in special
In thin array, after a pleasant guise,
  When her loose gown from her shoulders did fall,
  And she me caught in her arms long and small,
    There with all sweetly did me kiss,
    And softly said: 'Dear heart, how like you this?'

It was no dream; I lay broad waking:
  But all is turned thorough my gentleness
Into a strange fashion of forsaking;
  And I have leave to go of her goodness;
  And she also to use new-fangleness.
    But since that I so kindly am served,
    I fain would know what she hath deserved.

*

    And wilt thou leave me thus?
      Say nay, say nay, for shame,
      To save thee from the blame
      Of all my grief and grame;
    And wilt thou leave me thus?
      Say nay, say nay!

    And wilt thou leave me thus
      That hath loved thee so long
      In wealth and woe among?
      And is thy heart so strong
    As for to leave me thus?
      Say nay, say nay!

20

And wilt thou leave me thus,
  That hath given thee my heart
  Never for to depart
  Neither for pain or smart:
And wilt thou leave me thus?
    Say nay, say nay!

And wilt thou leave me thus,
  And have no more pity
  Of him that loveth thee?
  Helas thy cruelty!
And wilt thou leave me thus?
    Say nay, say nay!

*

A face that should content me wonderous well
Should not be fair but lovely to behold,
With gladsome cheer all grief for to expel;
With sober looks so would I that it should
Speak without words such words as none can tell;
Her tress also should be of crisped gold;
With wit: and thus might chance I might be tied,
And knit again the knot that should not slide.

HENRY HOWARD, EARL OF SURREY

1517–1547

When raging love with extreme pain
Most cruelly distrains my heart,
When that my tears, as floods of rain,
Bear witness of my woeful smart,
When sighs have wasted so my breath
That I lie at the point of death:

I call to mind the navy great
That the Greeks brought to Troye town,
And how the boisterous winds did beat
Their ships, and rent their sails adown,
Till Agamemnon's daughter's blood
Appeased the gods that them withstood:

And how that in those ten years' war
Full many a bloody deed was done,
And many a lord that came full far
There caught his bane, alas, too soon,
And many a good knight overrun,
Before the Greeks had Helen won.

Then think I thus: 'Sith such repair,
So long time war of valiant men,
Was all to win a lady fair,
Shall I not learn to suffer then?
And to think my life well spent to be
Serving a worthier wight than she?'

Therefore I never shall repent,
But pains, contented, still endure;
Foe like as when, rough winter spent,
The pleasant spring straight draweth in ure;
So, after raging storms of care,
Joyful at length may be my fare.

*

Brittle beauty, that Nature made so frail,
Whereof the gift is small, and short the season,
Flowering today, tomorrow apt to fail,
Fickle treasure, abhorred of reason,
Dangerous to deal with, vain, of none avail,
Costly in keeping, past not worth two peason,
Slipper in sliding as is an eel's tail,
Hard to obtain, once gotten not geason,

22

Jewel of jeopardy that peril doth assail,
False and untrue, enticed oft to treason,
Enemy to youth: that most may I bewail!
Ah, bitter sweet, infecting as the poison!
Thou farest as fruit that with the frost is taken:
Today ready ripe, tomorrow all to shaken.

THOMAS CAMPION

1540–1581

Follow, follow,
Though with mischief
Arm'd, like whirlwind
Now she flies thee;
Time can conquer
Love's unkindness;
Love can alter
Time's disgraces:
Till death faint not
Then, but follow.
Could I catch that
Nimble traitor
Scornful Laura,
Swift-foot Laura,
Soon then would I
Seek avengement
What's th' avengement?
Ev'n submissly
Prostrate then to
Beg for mercy.

Rose-cheekt Laura, come
Sing thou smoothly with thy beauty's
Silent music, either other
　　　　Sweetly gracing.
Lovely forms do flow
From concent divinely framed;
Heav'n is music, and thy beauty's
　　　　Birth is heavenly.

These dull notes we sing
Discords need for helps to grace them,
Only beauty purely loving
　　　　Knows no discord.

But still moves delight,
Like clear springs renew'd by flowing,
Ever perfect, ever in them-
　　　　selves eternal.

*

Thrice toss these oaken ashes in the air,
Thrice sit thou mute in this inchanted chair;
And thrice three times tie up this true loves knot,
And murmur soft, she will, or she will not.

Go burn these pois'nous weeds in yon blue fire,
These screech-owl's feathers and this prickling briar;
This cypress gathered at a dead man's grave;
That all thy fears and cares an end may have.

Then come, you Fairies, dance with me a round;
Melt her hard heart with your melodious sound:
In vain are all the charms I can devise:
She hath an art to break them with her eyes.

*

Shall I come, if I swim? wide are the waves, you see:
Shall I come, if I fly, my dear love, to thee?
Streams Venus will appease; Cupid gives me wings;
All the powers assist my desire
Save you alone, that set my woful heart on fire.

You are fair, so was Hero that in Sestos dwelt;
She a priest, yet the heat of love truly felt.
A greater stream than this did her love divide;
But she was his guide with a light:
So through the streams Leander did enjoy her sight.

*

When thou must home to shades of under ground,
And there arriv'd a new admired guest,
The beautious spirits do ingirt thee round,
White Iope, blith Hellen, and the rest,
To hear the stories of thy finisht love
From that smooth tongue whose music hell can move;

Then wilt thou speak of banqueting delights,
Of masks and revels which sweet youth did make,
Of turnies and great challenges of knights,
And all these triumphs for thy beauty's sake:
When thou hast told these honours done to thee,
Then tell, O tell, how thou didst murther me.

*

Thou art not fair for all thy red and white,
For all those rosy ornaments in thee;
Thou art not sweet, though made of mere delight,
Nor fair nor sweet, unless thou pity me.
I will not soothe thy fancies: thou shalt prove
That beauty is no beauty without love.

Yet love not me, nor seek thou to allure
My thoughts with beauty; were it more divine,
Thy smiles and kisses I cannot endure,
I'll not be wrapt up in those arms of thine,
Now shew it if thou be a woman right,—
Embrace, and kiss, and love me, in despite.

*

Follow your saint, follow with accents sweet;
Haste you, sad notes, fall at her flying feet:
There, wrapped in cloud of sorrow, pity move,
And tell the ravisher of my soul I perish for her love.
But if she scorns my never-ceasing pain,
Then burst with sighing in her sight and ne'er return again.

All that I sang still to her praise did tend,
Still she was first; still she my songs did end.
Yet she my love and music both doth fly,
The music that her Echo is and beauty's sympathy;
Then let my notes pursue her scornful flight:
It shall suffice that they were breath'd and died for her delight.

*

Follow thy fair sun, unhappy shadow,
Though thou be black as night,
And she made all of light
Yet follow thy fair sun, unhappy shadow.

Follow her whose light thy light depriveth,
Though here thou liv'st disgraced,
And she in heaven is placed,
Yet follow her whose light the world reviveth.

Follow those pure beams whose beauty burneth,
That so have scorched thee,
As thou still black must be,
Till her kind beams thy black to brightness turneth.

26

Follow her while yet her glory shineth:
There comes a luckless night,
That will dim all her light;
And this the black unhappy shade divineth.

Follow still since so thy fates ordained,
The sun must have his shade,
Till both at once do fade,
The sun still proud, the shadow still disdained.

SIR WALTER RALEIGH

1552–1618

As you came from the holy land
    Of Walsinghame,
Met you not with my true love
    By the way as you came?

How shall I know your true love
    That have met many one,
As I went to the holy land,
    That have come, that have gone?

She is neither white nor brown,
    But as the heavens fair;
There is none hath a form so divine
    In the earth or the air.

Such a one did I meet, good sir,
    Such an angelic face,
Who like a queen, like a nymph, did appear,
    By her gate, by her grace.

She hath left me here all alone,
    All alone, as unknown,
Who sometimes did me lead with herself,
    And me loved as her own.

What's the cause that she leaves you alone,
    And a new way doth take,
Who loved you once as her own,
    And her joy did you make?

I have loved her all my youth,
    But now old, as you see,
Love likes not the falling fruit
    From the withered tree.

Know that love is a careless child,
    And forgets promise past;
He is blind, he is deaf when he list,
    And in faith never fast.

His desire is a dureless content,
    And a trustless joy;
He is won with a world of despair,
    And lost with a toy.

Of womankind such indeed is the love,
    Or the word love abused,
Under which many childish desires
    And conceits are excused.

But true love is a durable fire,
    In the mind ever burning,
Never sick, never old, never dead,
    From itself never turning.

With how sad steps, O Moon! thou climb'st the skies!
　How silently, and with how wan a face!
　What! may it be that even in heavenly place
That busy archer his sharp arrows tries?
Sure, if that long-with-love-acquainted eyes
　Can judge of love, thou feel'st a lover's case.
　I read it in thy looks. Thy languisht grace
To me that feel the like, thy state descries.
　Then even of fellowship, O Moon, tell me
Is constant love deemed there but want of wit?
　Are beauties there as proud as here they be?
Do they above love to be loved, and yet
　Those lovers scorn whom that love doth possess?
　Do they call virtue there, ungratefulness?

*

　　　When, to my deadly pleasure,
　　　When to my lively torment,
　　　Lady, mine eyes remained
　　　Joined, alas, to your beams.

　　　With violence of heavenly
　　　Beauty tied to virtue,
　　　Reason abashed retired;
　　　Gladly my senses yielded.

　　　They to the beamy suns went,
　　　Where by the death of all deaths
　　　Find to what harm they hastened.

29

Yet, yet, a life to their death,
Lady, you have reserved!
Lady, the life of love!

For though my sense be from me
And I be dead, who want sense;
Yet do we both live in you!

Thus do I fall to rise thus,
Thus do I die to live thus,
Chained to a change, I change not.

Thus may I not be from you!
Thus be my senses on you!
Thus what I think is of you!
Thus what I seek is in you!
    All what I am, it is you!

*

Ah bed! the field where joy's peace some do see;
   The field where all my thoughts to war be trained:
How is thy grace by my strange fortune stained!
How thy ice shores by my sighs stormed be!
With sweet soft shades, thou oft invitest me
   To steal some rest; but, wretch! I am constrained—
   Spurred with Love's spur, though gold; and shortly reined
With Care's hard hand—to turn and toss in thee!
   While the black horrors of the silent night
   Paint Woe's black face so lively to my sight;
That tedious leisure marks each wrinkled line.
   But when Aurora leads out Phoebus' dance,
   Mine eyes then only wink: for spite, perchance,
That worms should have their sun and I want mine.

Whenas the rye reach to the chin,
And chopcherry, chopcherry ripe within,
Strawberries swimming in the cream,
And school-boys playing in the stream;
Then O, then O, then O, my true-love said,
Till that time come again
She could not live a maid.

ANONYMOUS

(WILLIAM BYRD'S *Songs of Sundrie Natures*, 1589)

I thought that Love had been a boy
          With blinded eyes,
Or else some other wanton toy
          That men devise,
Like tales of fairies often told
By doting age that dies for cold.

Constant Penelope sends to thee, careless Ulysses!
Write not again but come, sweet Mate, thyself to revive me.
Troy we do much envy, we desolate ladies of Greece.
Not Priamus, nor yet all Troy, can us recompense make.
Oh, that he had, when he first took shipping to Lacedemon,
That adulterer I mean, had been o'erwhelmed with waters!
Then had I not lien now all alone, thus quivering for cold;
Nor used this complaint, nor have thought the day to be so long.

ANONYMOUS

(WILLIAM BYRD'S *Second Book of Songs and Sonnets*, 1611)

Crowned with flowers, I saw fair Amarillis,
  By Thirsis sit, hard by a fount of crystal,
And with her hand more white than snow or lilies
  On sand she wrote, 'My faith shall be immortal';
    And suddenly a storm of wind and weather
    Blew all her faith and sand away together.

Dear, if you change, I'll never choose again;
Sweet, if you shrink, I'll never think of love;
Fair, if you fail, I'll judge all beauty vain;
Wise, if too weak, more wits I'll never prove.
    Dear, sweet, fair, wise, change, shrink, nor be not weak;
    And, on my faith, my faith shall never break.

Earth with her flowers shall sooner heaven adorn;
Heaven her bright stars, through earth's dim globe shall move.
Fire, heat shall lose; and frosts of flames be born;
Air made to shine, as black as hell shall prove:
    Earth, heaven, fire, air, the world transformed shall view,
    Ere I prove false to faith, or strange to you.

I saw my Lady weep,
And Sorrow proud to be advanced so
In those fair eyes, where all perfections keep;
    Her face was full of woe,
But such a woe (believe me) as wins more hearts
Than mirth can do, with her enticing parts.

Sorrow was there made fair,
And Passion, wise; Tears, a delightful thing;
Silence, beyond all speech, a wisdom rare;
  She made her sighs to sing,
And all things with so sweet a sadness move;
As made my heart both grieve and love.

O Fairer than aught else
The world can shew, leave off, in time, to grieve,
Enough, enough! Your joyful look excels;
  Tears kill the heart, believe,
O strive not to be excellent in woe,
Which only breeds your beauty's overthrow.

ANONYMOUS

(JOHN DOWLAND's *Third Book of Songs or Airs*, 1603)

Weep you no more, sad fountains,
  What need you flow so fast?
Look how the snowy mountains
  Heaven's sun doth gently waste.
But my sun's heavenly eyes
  View not your weeping,
  That now lies sleeping
Softly! now softly lies sleeping!

Sleep is a reconciling,
  A rest that peace begets;
Doth not the sun rise smiling,
  When fair at e'en he sets?
Rest you then, rest, sad eyes!
  Melt not in weeping,
  While she lies sleeping
Softly! now softly lies sleeping!

Farewell, Unkind! Farewell! to me, no more a father!
Since my heart holds my Love most dear;
The wealth, which thou dost reap, another's hand must gather.
    Though thy heart still lies buried there!
Then farewell, O farewell! Welcome, my Love, welcome my joy
    for ever!
'Tis not the vain desire of human fleeting beauty
Makes my mind to live, though my means do die.
Nor do I Nature wrong, though I forget my duty;
Love, not in the blood, but in the spirit doth lie!
Then farewell, O farewell! Welcome, my Love, welcome my joy
    for ever!

*

Time stands still, with gazing on her face!
Stand still, and gaze! for minutes, hours and years, to her give place.
All other things shall change, but She remains the same,
Till heavens changed have their course, and Time hath lost his name.
Cupid doth hover up and down, blinded with her fair eyes!
And Fortune captive at her feet, contemned and conquered lies!

Henry Constable

1562–1613

Hope, like the hyaena, coming to be old,
    Alters his shape; is turned into Despair.
Pity my hoary hopes! Maid of Clear Mould!
    Think not that frowns can ever make thee fair.
What harm is it to kiss, to laugh, to play?
    Beauty's no blossom, if it be not used.

Sweet dalliance keeps the wrinkles long away:
  Repentance follows them that have refused.
To bring you to the knowledge of your good
  I seek, I sue. O try, and then believe!
Each image can be chaste that's carved of wood.
  You show you live when men you do relieve.
Iron with wearing shines. Rust wasteth treasure.
On earth, but love there is no other pleasure.

JOSHUA SYLVESTER

1563–1618

Sweet mouth, that send'st a musky-rosed breath;
Fountain of nectar and delightful balm;
Eyes cloudy-clear, smile-frowning, stormy-calm;
Whose every glance darts me a living-death
Brows, bending quaintly your round ebene arks;
Smile, that than Venus sooner Mars besots;
Locks more than golden, curl'd in curious knots,
Where, in close ambush, wanton Cupid lurks;
Grace Angel-like; fair fore-head, smooth, and high;
Pure white, that dimm'st the lilies of the vale;
Vermilion rose, that mak'st Aurora pale:
Rare spirit, to rule this beautious Emperie:
  If in your force, divine effects I view,
    Ah, who can blame me, if I worship you?

MICHAEL DRAYTON

1563–1631

Since there's no help, come, let us kiss and part,
Nay, I have done: you get no more of me,
And I am glad, yea glad with all my heart,
That thus so cleanly, I myself can free.
Shake hands for ever, cancel all our vows,
And, when we meet at any time again,
Be it not seen in either of our brows
That we one jot of former love retain.
Now at the last gasp of Love's latest breath,
When, his pulse failing, passion speechless lies,
When Faith is kneeling by his bed of death,
And Innocence is closing up his eyes,
 Now if thou wouldst, when all have given him over,
 From death to life, thou might'st him yet recover.

*

How many paltry foolish painted things,
That now in coaches trouble ev'ry street
Shall be forgotten, whom no poet sings,
Ere they be well wrap'd in their winding sheet?
Where I to thee eternitie shall give,
When nothing else remaineth of these days,
And Queens hereafter shall be glad to live
Upon the alms of thy superfluous praise.
Virgins and matrons, reading these my rhymes,
Shall be so much delighted with thy story,
That they shall grieve they lived not in these times,
To have seen Thee, their sex's only glory:
 So shalt thou fly above the vulgar throng,
 Still to survive in my immortal song.

How like a winter hath my absence beene
From thee, the pleasure of the fleeting yeare!
What freezings have I felt, what darke daies seene!
What old December's barenesse every where!
And yet this time remov'd was sommer's time,
The teeming autumne big with ritch increase,
Bearing the wanton burthen of the prime,
Like widdowed wombs after their Lord's decease:
Yet this aboundant issue seem'd to me,
But hope of Orphans, and un-fathered fruite,
For sommer and his pleasures waite on thee,
And thou away, the very birds are mute.
  Or if they sing, tis with so dull a cheere,
    That leaves looke pale, dreading the winter's neere.

*

Let me not to the marriage of true mindes
Admit impediments, love is not love
Which alters when it alteration findes,
Or bends with the remover to remove.
O no, it is an ever fixed marke
That lookes on tempests and is never shaken;
It is the star to every wandering barke,
Whose worth's unknowne, although his height be taken.
Love's not Time's foole, though rosie lips and cheeks
Within his bending sickle's compasse come,
Love alters not with his breefe houres and weekes,
But beares it out even to the edge of doome:
  If this be error and upon me proved,
    I never writ, nor no man ever loved.

When in the chronicle of wasted time,
I see descriptions of the fairest wights,
And beautie making beautiful old rime,
In praise of Ladies dead, and lovely Knights,
Then in the blazon of sweet beauty's best,
Of hand, of foote, of lip, of eye, of brow,
I see their antique pen would have exprest
Even such a beauty as you maister now.
So all their praises are but prophecies
Of this our time, all you prefiguring,
And for they look'd but with devining eyes,
They had not skill enough your worth to sing:
    For we which now behold these present dayes,
    Have eyes to wonder, but lack toungs to praise.

*

That time of year thou maist in me behold,
When yellow leaves, or none, or few doe hange
Upon those boughs which shake against the cold,
Bare ruin'd quiers, where late the sweet birds sang.
In me thou seest the twi-light of such day,
As after sun-set fadeth in the west,
Which by and by blacke night doth take away,
Death's second selfe that seals up all in rest.
In me thou seest the glowing of such fire,
That on the ashes of his youth doth lye,
As the death bed, whereon it must expire,
Consum'd with that which it was nurrisht by.
    This thou percev'st, which makes thy love more strong,
    To love that well, which thou must leave ere long.

*

When I have seen by time's fell hand defaced
The rich proud cost of outworne buried age,
When sometime loftie towers I see downe rased,
And brasse eternall slave to mortall rage,

39

When I have seene the hungry Ocean gaine
Advantage on the kingdom of the shoare,
And the firme soile win of the watry maine,
Increasing store with losse, and losse with store,
When I have seen such interchange of state,
Or state itselfe confounded, to decay,
Ruine hath taught me thus to ruminate
That Time will come and take my love away.
    This thought is as a death which cannot choose
    But weepe to have that which it feares to loose.

*

Shall I compare thee to a Summer's day?
Thou art more lovely and more temperate:
Rough windes do shake the darling buds of Maie,
And Summer's lease hath all too short a date:
Sometimes too hot the eye of heaven shines,
And often is his gold complexion dimm'd,
And every faire from faire some-time declines,
By chance, or nature's changing course untrim'd:
But thy eternall Summer shall not fade,
Nor loose possession of that faire thou ow'st,
Nor shall death brag thou wandr'st in his shade,
When in eternall lines to time thou grow'st,
    So long as men can breathe or eyes can see,
    So long lives this, and this gives life to thee.

*

How should I your true love know
    From another one?
By his cockle hat and staff,
    And his sandal shoon.

He is dead and gone, lady,
    He is dead and gone;
At his head a grass-green turf;
    At his heels a stone.

40

White his shroud as the mountain snow,
  Larded with sweet flowers;
Which bewept to the grave did go
  With true-love showers.

*

To-morrow is Saint Valentine's day,
  All in the morning betime,
And I a maid at your window,
  To be your Valentine:
Then up he rose, and donn'd his clothes,
  And dupp'd the chamber-door;
Let in the maid, that out a maid
  Never departed more.

By Gis and by Saint Charity,
  Alack, and fie for shame!
Young men will do't, if they come to't;
  By Cock they are to blame.
Quoth she, before you tumbled me,
  You promis'd me to wed:
So would I ha' done, by yonder sun,
  An thou hadst not come to my bed.

SIR HENRY WOTTON
1568–1639

UPON THE DEATH OF SIR ALBERT MORTON'S
WIFE

He first deceased; she for a little tried
To live without him, liked it not, and died.

You meaner beauties of the night,
    That poorly satisfy our eyes
More by your number than your light,
    You common people of the skies;
    Where are you when the moon shall rise?

You curious chanters of the wood,
    That warble forth Dame Nature's lays,
Thinking your passions understood
    By your weak accents; what's your praise,
    When Philomel her voice shall raise?

You violets that first appear,
    By your pure purple mantles known
Like the proud virgins of the year,
    As if the spring were all your own;
    What are you when the rose is blown?

So, when my mistress shall be seen
    In form and beauty of her mind,
By virtue first, then choice, a Queen,
    Tell me if she were not designed
    The eclipse and glory of her kind?

BARNABE BARNES

1569–1609

Soft, lovely, rose-like lips, conjoined with mine,
    Breathing out precious incense such,
(Such as, at Paphos, smokes to Venus' shrine)
    Making my lips immortal with their touch,

My cheeks, with touch of thy soft cheeks divine,
   Thy soft warm cheeks which Venus favours much;
Those arms, such arms, which me embraced,
   Me with immortal cincture girding round,
   Of everlasting bliss, then bound
With her enfolded thighs in mine entangled,
And both in one self-soul placed,
   Made a hermaphrodite with pleasure ravished.
There heat for heat's, soul for soul's empire wrangled;
   Why died not I with love so largely lavished?
For waked (not finding truth of dreams before)
It secret vexeth ten times more.

*

O Powers Celestial, with what sophistry
Took She delight to blank my heart by sorrow!
And in such riddles act my tragedy:
Making this day for him; for me, tomorrow.
   Where shall I Sonnets borrow?
Where shall I find breasts, sighs, and tongue,
Which my great wrongs might to the world dispense?
   Where my defence?
My physic, where? For how can I live long
That have foregone my Heart? I'll steal from hence,
From restless souls, mine hymns; from seas, my tears;
From winds, my sighs; from concave rocks and steel,
My sighs' and voice's echo; reeds which feel
Calm blasts still moving, which the shepherd bears
   For wailing plaints, my tongue shall be!
The land unknown, to rest and comfort me.

TO THE MOST BEAUTIFUL LADY,
THE LADY BRIDGET MANNERS

Rose of that Garland! fairest and sweetest
Of all those sweet and fair flowers!
Pride of chaste Cynthia's rich crown!
Receive this Verse, thy matchless beauty meetest.
Behold thy graces which thou greetest,
 And all the secret powers
Of thine, and suchlike beauties, here set down.
Here shalt thou find thy frown!
 Here thy sunny smiling!
Fame's plumes fly with thy Love's, which should be fleetest!
 Here, my loves' tempests and showers!
These, read, sweet Beauty, whom my Muse shall crown!
Who for thee such a garland is compiling
 Of so divine scents and colours,
And is immortal, Time beguiling!

BEN JONSON
1572–1637

THE HOUR-GLASS

Do but consider this small dust, here running in the glass,
  By atoms moved.
Could you believe that this the body was
  Of one that loved?
And in his mistress' flame playing like a fly,
  Turned to cinders by her eye?
Yes, and in death as life unblest,
  To have't expressed,
Even ashes of lovers find no rest.

TO CELIA

Drink to me only with thine eyes,
   And I will pledge with mine;
Or leave a kiss within the cup,
   And I'll not look for wine.
The thirst that from the soul doth rise,
   Doth ask a drink divine;
But might I of Jove's nectar sup,
   I would not change for thine.

I sent thee late a rosy wreath,
   Not so much honouring thee,
As giving it a hope that there
   It could not withered be.
But thou thereon didst only breathe,
   And sent'st it back to me;
Since when it grows, and smells, I swear,
   Not of itself, but thee.

JOHN DONNE

1572–1631

THE FUNERALL

Who ever comes to shroud me, do not harme
   Nor question much
That subtile wreath of haire, which crowns my arme;
The mystery, the signe you must not touch,
   For 'tis my outward Soule,
Viceroy to that, which then to heaven being gone,
   Will leave this to controule,
And keep these limbes, her Provinces, from dissolution.

For if the sinewie thread my braine lets fall
   Through every part,
Can tye those parts, and make mee one of all;
These haires which upward grew, and strength and art
   Have from a better braine,
Can better do't; Except she meant that I
   By this should know my pain,
As prisoners then are manacled, when they're condemn'd to die.

What ere shee meant by't, bury it with me,
   For since I am
Loves martyr, it might breed idolatrie,
If into others hands these Reliques came;
   As 'twas humility
To afford to it all that a Soule can doe,
   So, 'tis some bravery,
That since you would have none of mee, I bury some of you.

THE EXTASIE

Where, like a pillow on a bed
   A Pregnant banke swel'd up, to rest
The violets reclining head,
   Sat we two, one anothers best.
Our hands were firmely cimented
   By a fast balme, which thence did spring,
Our eye-beames twisted, and did thred
   Our eyes, upon one double string;
So t'entergraft our hands, as yet
   Was all the meanes to make us one,
And pictures in our eyes to get
   Was all our propagation
As 'twixt two equall Armies, Fate
   Suspends uncertaine victorie,
Our soules, (which to advance their state,
   Were gone out,) hung 'twixt her, and mee.

And whilst our soules negotiate there,
   Wee like sepulchrall statues lay;
All day, the same our postures were,
   And we said nothing, all the day.
If any, so by love refin'd,
   That he soules language understood,
And by good love were growen all minde,
   Within convenient distance stood,
He (though he knew not which soul spake,
   Because both meant, both spake the same)
Might thence a new concoction take,
   And part far purer than he came.
This Extasie doth unperplex
   (We said) and tell us what we love,
We see by this, it was not sexe,
   Wee see, we saw not what did move:
But as all severall soules containe
   Mixture of things, they know not what,
Love, these mixt soules, doth mixe againe,
   And makes both one, each this and that.
A single violet transplant,
   The strength, the colour, and the size,
(All which before was poore, and scant,)
   Redoubles still, and multiplies.
When love, with one another so
   Interinanimates two soules,
That abler soule, which thence doth flow,
   Defects of lonelinesse controles.
Wee then, who are this new soule, know,
   Of what we are compos'd, and made,
For, th'Atomies of which we grow,
   Are soules, whom no change can invade.
But O alas, so long, so farre
   Our bodies why do we forbeare?
They are ours, though they are not wee; Wee are
   The intelligences, they the spheres.
We owe them thankes, because they thus,
   Did us, to us, at first convay,

Yeelded their forces, sense, to us,
   Nor are drosse to us, but allay.
On man heavens influence works not so,
   But that it first imprints the ayre,
So soule into the soule may flow,
   Though it to body first repaire.
As our blood labours to beget
   Spirits, as like soules as it can,
Because such fingers need to knit
   That subtle knot, which makes us man:
So must pure lovers soules descend
   T'affections, and to faculties,
Which sense may reach and apprehend,
   Else a great Prince in prison lies.
T'our bodies turne wee then, that so
   Weake men on love reveal'd may looke;
Loves mysteries in soules doe grow,
   But yet the body is his booke.
And if some lover, such as wee,
   Have heard this dialogue of one,
   Let him still marke us, he shall see
   Small change, when we're to bodies gone.

THE APPARITION

When by thy scorne, O murdresse I am dead,
And that thou thinkst thee free
From all solicitation from mee,
Then shall my ghost come to thy bed,
And thee, fain'd vestall, in worse armes shall see;
Then thy sicke taper will begin to winke,
And he, whose thou art then, being tyr'd before,
Will, if thou stirre, or pinch to wake him, thinke
   Thou call'st for more,
And in false sleepe will from thee shrinke,
And then poore Aspen wretch, neglected thou

48

Bath'd in a cold quicksilver sweat wilt lye
    A veryer ghost than I;
What will I say, I will not tell thee now,
Lest that preserve thee; and since my love is spent,
I had rather thou shouldst painfully repent,
Than by my threatenings rest still innocent.

TWICKNAM GARDEN

Blasted with sighs, and surrounded with teares,
    Hither I come to seeke the spring,
    And in mine eyes, and at mine eares,
Receive such balmes, as else cure every thing;
    But O, selfe traytor, I do bring
The spider love, which transubstantiates all,
    And can convert Manna to gall,
And that this place may thoroughly be thought
    True Paradise, I have the serpent brought.

'Twere wholsomer for mee, that winter did
    Benight the glory of this place,
    And that a grave frost did forbid
These trees to laugh, and mocke mee to my face;
    But that I may not this disgrace
Indure, nor yet leave loving, Love let mee
    Some senslesse peece of this place bee;
Make me a mandrake, so I may groane here,
    Or a stone fountaine weeping out my yeare.

Hither with christall vyals, lovers come,
    And take my teares, which are loves wine,
    And try your mistresse Teares at home,
For all are false, that tast not just like mine;
    Alas, hearts do not in eyes shine,
Nor can you more judge womans thoughts by teares,
    Than by her shadow, what she weares.
O perverse sexe, where none is true but shee,
    Who's therefore true, because her truth kills mee.

49

THE CANONIZATION

For Godsake hold your tongue, and let me love,
  Or chide my palsie, or my gout,
My five gray haires, or ruin'd fortune flout,
    With wealth your state, your minde with Arts improve,
      Take you a course, get you a place,
      Observe his honour, or his grace,
Or the Kings reall, or his stamped face
  Contemplate, what you will, approve,
  So you will let me love.

Alas, alas, who's injur'd by my love?
  What merchants ships have my sighs drown'd?
Who saies my teares have overflow'd his ground?
    When did my colds a forward spring remove?
      When did the heats which my veines fill
      Adde one more to the plaguie Bill?
Soldiers finde warres, and Lawyers finde out still
  Litigious men, which quarrels move,
  Though she and I do love.

Call us what you will, wee are made such by love;
  Call her one, mee another flye,
We're Tapers too, and at our owne cost die,
    And wee in us finde th'Eagle and the Dove.
      The Phoenix riddle hath more wit
      By us, we two being one, are it.
So to one neutral thing both sexes fit,
  Wee dye and rise the same, and prove
  Mysterious by this love.

Wee can dye by it, if not live by love,
  And if unfit for tombes and hearse
Our legend bee, it will be fit for verse;
    And if no peece of Chronicle wee prove,

We'll build in sonnets pretty roomes;
    As well a well wrought urne becomes
The greatest ashes, as half-acre tombes,
    And by these hymnes, all shall approve
    Us *Canoniz'd* for Love:

And thus invoke us; You whom reverend love
    Made one anothers hermitage;
You, to whom love was peace, that now is rage;
    Who did the whole worlds soule contract, and drove
        Into the glasses of your eyes
        (So made such mirrors, and such spies,
That they did all to you epitomize,)
    Countries, Townes, Courts: Beg from above
    A patterne of your love!

THE GOOD-MORROW

I wonder by my troth, what thou and I
Did, till we lov'd? were we not wean'd till then?
But suck'd on country pleasures, childishly?
Or snorted we in the seven sleepers den?
'Twas so; But this, all pleasures fancies bee.
If ever any beauty I did see,
Which I desir'd, and got, t'was but a dreame of thee.

And now good morrow to our waking soules,
Which watch not one another out of feare;
For love, all love of other sights controules,
And makes one little roome, an every where.
Let sea-discoverers to new worlds have gone,
Let Maps to other worlds on worlds have showne,
Let us possesse one world, each hath one, and is one.

My face in thine eye, thine in mine appeares,
And true plain hearts doe in the faces rest,
Where can we finde two better hemispheares
Without sharpe North, without declining West?
Whatever dyes, was not mixt equally;
If our two loves be one, or thou and I
Love so alike, that none do slacken, none can die.

JOHN FLETCHER

1579–1625

Take, oh take those lips away,
 That so sweetly were forsworn,
And those eyes, the break of day,
 Lights that do mislead the morn.
But my kisses bring again,
Seals of love, but sealed in vain.

Hide, oh hide those hills of snow,
 Which thy frozen bosom bears,
On whose tops the pinks that grow
 Are yet of those that April wears.
But first set my poor heart free,
Bound in those icy chains by thee.

    (First stanza in *Measure for Measure*
      [W. Shakespeare], Act IV, Sc. 1)

*

My man Thomas
Did me promise
He would visit me this night.

I am here, love;
Tell me, dear love,
How I may obtain thy sight.

Come up to my window, love;
Come, come, come:
Come to my window, my dear;
The wind nor the rain
Shall trouble thee again,
But thou shalt be lodged here.

EDWARD HERBERT, LORD CHERBURY

1583–1648

KISSING

Come hither, womankind and all their worth,
Give me thy kisses as I call them forth.
Give me the billing kiss, that of the dove,
    A kiss of love;
The melting kiss, a kiss that doth consume
    To a perfume;
The extract kiss, of every sweet a part,
    A kiss of art;
The kiss which ever stirs some new delight,
    A kiss of might;
The twaching smacking kiss, and when you cease,
    A kiss of peace;
The music kiss, crochet-and-quaver time;
    The kiss of rhyme;
The kiss of eloquence, which doth belong
    Unto the tongue;
The kiss of all the sciences in one,
    The Kiss alone.
So, 'tis enough.

STOLEN PLEASURE

My sweet did sweetly sleep,
And on her rosy face
Stood tears of pearl, which beauty's self did weep;
I, wond'ring at her grace,
Did all amaz'd remain,
When Love said, 'Fool, can looks thy wishes crown?
Time past comes not again.'
Then did I me bow down,
And kissing her fair breast, lips, cheeks, and eyes,
Prov'd here on earth the joys of paradise.

KISSES DESIRED

Though I with strange desire
To kiss those rosy lips am set on fire,
Yet will I cease to crave
Sweet touches in such store,
As he who long before
From Lesbia them in thousands did receive.
Heart mine, but once me kiss,
And I by that sweet bliss
Even swear to cease you to importune more;
Poor one no number is;
Another word of me ye shall not hear
After one kiss, but still one kiss, my dear.

UPON JULIA'S CLOTHES

Whenas in silks my Julia goes,
Then, then, methinks, how sweetly flows
The liquefaction of her clothes.

Next, when I cast mine eyes and see
That brave vibration each way free,
O how that glittering taketh me!

THE MAD MAID'S SONG

Good-morrow to the day so fair,
  Good-morning, sir, to you;
Good-morrow to mine own torn hair,
  Bedabbled in the dew.

Good-morning to this primrose too,
  Good-morrow to each maid
That will with flowers the tomb bestrew
  Wherein my love is laid.

Ah! woe is me, woe, woe, is me,
  Alack and well-a-day;
For pity, sir, find out that bee
  Which bore my love away.

I'll seek him in your bonnet brave,
  I'll seek him in your eyes;
Nay, now I think th'ave made his grave
  I'th'bed of strawberries.

I'll seek him there; I know ere this
  The cold, cold earth doth shake him;
But I will go or send a kiss
  By you, sir, to awake him.

Pray, hurt him not; though he be dead,
  He knows well who do love him,
And who with green turfs rear his head,
  And who do rudely move him.

He's soft and tender (pray take heed);
  With bands of cowslips bind him,
And bring him home; but 'tis decreed
  That I shall never find him.

CHOP-CHERRY

Thou gav'st me leave to kiss,
  Thou gav'st me leave to woo;
Thou mad'st me think, by this
  And that, thou lov'st me too.

But I shall ne'er forget
  How, for to make thee merry
Thou mad'st me chop, but yet
  Another snapp'd the cherry.

TO THE VIRGINS, TO MAKE MUCH OF TIME

Gather ye rosebuds while ye may,
  Old time is still a-flying:
And this same flower that smiles today
  Tomorrow will be dying.

The glorious lamp of heaven, the sun,
   The higher he's a-getting,
The sooner will his race be run,
   And nearer he's to setting.

That age is best which is the first,
   When youth and blood are warmer;
But being spent, the worse, and worst
   Times still succeed the former.

Then be not coy, but use your time,
   And while ye may, go marry:
For having lost but once your prime
   You may for ever tarry.

DELIGHT IN DISORDER

A sweet disorder in the dress
Kindles in clothes a wantonness:
A lawn about the shoulders thrown
Into a fine distraction:
An erring lace which here and there
Enthralls the crimson stomacher:
A cuff neglectful, and thereby
Ribbons to flow confusedly:
A winning wave, deserving note,
In the tempestuous petticoat:
A careless shoe-string, in whose tie
I see a wild civility:
Do more bewitch me than when art
Is too precise in every part.

SONNET

Tell me no more how fair she is,
   I have no minde to hear
The story of that distant bliss
   I never shall come near:
By sad experience I have found
That her perfection is my wound.

And tell me not how fond I am
   To tempt my daring Fate,
From whence no triumph ever came,
   But to repent too late:
There is some hope ere long I may
In silence dote myself away.

I ask no pity (Love) from thee,
   Nor will thy justice blame,
So that thou wilt not envy mee
   The glory of my flame:
Which crowns my heart whene'er it dyes,
In that it falls her sacrifice.

UPON A BRAID OF HAIR IN A HEART

In this small Character is sent
My Loves eternal Monument.
Whilst we shall live, know, this chain'd Heart
Is our affections counter-part.
And if we never meet, think I
Bequeath'd it as my Legacy.

A SONG

Ask me no more where Jove bestows,
When June is past, the fading rose;
For in your beauty's orient deep
These flowers, as in their causes, sleep.

Ask me no more whither do stray
The golden atoms of the day;
For in pure love heaven did prepare
Those powders to enrich your hair.

Ask me no more whither doth haste
The nightingale, when May is past;
For in your sweet dividing throat
She winters, and keeps warm her note.

Ask me no more where those stars 'light,
That downwards fall in dead of night;
For in your eyes they sit, and there
Fixèd become, as in their sphere.

Ask me no more if east or west
The phoenix builds her spicy nest;
For unto you at last she flies,
And in your fragrant bosom dies.

TO MY INCONSTANT MISTRESS

When thou, poor excommunicate
  From all the joys of love, shalt see
The full reward and glorious fate
  Which my strong faith shall purchase me,
  Then curse thine own inconstancy.

A fairer hand than thine shall cure
  That heart, which thy false oaths did wound;
And to my soul a soul more pure
  Than thine shall by Love's hand be bound,
  And both with equal glory crown'd.

Then shalt thou weep, entreat, complain
  To Love, as I did once to thee;
When all thy tears shall be as vain
  As mine were then, for thou shalt be
  Damn'd for thy false apostacy.

LADY CATHERINE DYER

fl. 1630

EPITAPH ON THE MONUMENT OF
SIR WILLIAM DYER AT COLMWORTH, 1641

My dearest dust, could not thy hasty day
Afford thy drowszy patience leave to stay
One hower longer: so that we might either
Sate up, or gone to bedd together?
But since thy finisht labor hath possest
Thy weary limbs with early rest,

Enjoy it sweetly: and thy widdowe bride
Shall soone repose her by thy slumbring side.
Whose business, now, is only to prepare
My nightly dress, and call to prayre:
Mine eyes wax heavy and ye day growes cold.
Draw, draw ye closed curtaynes: and make room:
My deare, my dearest dust; I come, I come.

WILLIAM HABINGTON

1605–1654

TO ROSES IN THE BOSOM OF CASTARA

Ye, blushing Virgins! happy are
    In the chaste nunnery of her breasts;
For he'd profane so chaste a fair,
    Who e'er should call them Cupid's nests!

Transplanted thus, how bright ye grow!
    How rich a perfume do ye yield!
In some close garden, cowslips so
    Are sweeter than in th' open field.

In those white cloysters live secure
    From the rude blasts of wanton breath,
Each hour more inocent and pure,
    Till you shall wither into death.

Then, that which living gave you room,
    Your glorious sepulchre shall be;
There wants not marble for a tomb,
    Whose breast hath marble been to me.

UNDER A LADY'S PICTURE

Some ages hence, for it must not decay,
The doubtful wonderers at this piece will say,
Such Helen was! and who can blame the boy
That in so bright a flame consumed his Troy?
But, had like virtue shined in that fair Greek,
The amorous shepherd had not dared to seek
Or hope for pity; but with silent moan
And better fate, had perishèd alone.

*

Go, lovely Rose!
Tell her that wastes her time and me
That now she knows,
When I resemble her to thee,
How sweet and fair she seems to be.

Tell her that's young,
And shuns to have her graces spied,
That hadst thou sprung
In deserts, where no men abide,
Thou must have uncommended died.

Small is the worth
Of beauty from the light retired;
Bid her come forth,
Suffer herself to be desired,
And not blush so to be admired.

Then die! that she
The common fate of all things rare
May read in thee;
How small a part of time they share
That are so wondrous sweet and fair!

John Milton

1608–1674

Methought I saw my late espoused Saint
  Brought to me like Alcestis from the grave,
   Whom Joves great Son to her glad Husband gave,
  Rescu'd from death by force though pale and faint.
Mine as whom washt from spot of child-bed taint,
  Purification in the old Law did save,
  And such, as yet once more I trust to have
  Full sight of her in Heaven without restraint,
Came vested all in white, pure as her mind:
  Her face was vail'd, yet to my fancied sight,
  Love, sweetness, goodness, in her person shin'd
So clear, as in no face with more delight.
  But O as to embrace me she enclin'd
  I wak'd, she fled, and day brought back my night.

THE FIFTH ODE OF HORACE, LIB.I., RENDERED

What slender Youth bedew'd with liquid odours
Courts thee on Roses in some pleasant Cave,
    Pyrrha, for whom bind'st thou
    In wreaths thy golden Hair,

Plain in thy neatness; O how oft shall he
On Faith and changed Gods complain: and Seas
    Rough with black winds and storms
    Unwonted shall admire:
Who now enjoys thee credulous, all Gold,
Who always vacant, always amiable
    Hopes thee; of flattering gales
    Unmindfull. Hapless they
To whom thou untry'd seem'st fair. Me in my vow'd
Picture the sacred wall declares t'have hung
    My dank and dropping weeds
    To the stern God of Sea.

SIR JOHN SUCKLING

1609–1642

A SONG

Hast thou seen the Down in the Air,
    When wanton Blasts have tost it?
Or the Ship on the Sea
    When ruder Waves have crost it?
Hast thou mark'd the Crocodile's Weeping,
    Or the Fox's sleeping?
Or hast thou view'd the Peacock in his Pride,
    Or the Dove by his Bride,
    When he courts for his Leachery?
Oh! so fickle, oh! so vain, oh! so false, so false, is she!

SONG

Why so pale and wan, fond Lover?
    Prithee, why so pale?
Will, when looking well can't move her,
    Looking ill prevail?
    Prithee, why so pale?

Why so dull and mute, young Sinner?
    Prithee why so mute?
Will, when speaking well can't win her,
    Saying nothing do't?
    Prithee, why so mute?

Quit, quit for Shame! This will not move,
    This cannot take her;
If of herself she will not love,
    Nothing can make her:
    The Devil take her!

ABRAHAM COWLEY

1618–1667

EPITAPH

Underneath this Marble Stone,
Lie two Beauties join'd in one.

Two whose Loves Death could not sever,
For both liv'd, both dy'd together.

Two whose Souls, b'ing too divine
For Earth, in their own Sphere now shine.

Who have left their Loves to Fame,
And their Earth to Earth again.

RICHARD LOVELACE
1618–1658

THE SCRUTINIE

Why should you sweare I am forsworn,
    Since thine I vow'd to be?
Lady it is already morn,
    And 'twas last night I swore to thee
That fond impossibility.

Have I not lov'd thee much and long,
    A tedious twelve houres space?
I must all other Beauties wrong,
    And rob thee of a new imbrace;
Could I still dote upon thy Face.

Not, but all joy in thy browne haire,
    By others may be found;
But I must search the black and faire
    Like skilfull Mineralists that sound
For Treasure in un-plow'd-up ground.

Then, if when I have lov'd my round,
    Thou prov'st the pleasant she;
With spoyles of meaner Beauties crown'd,
    I laden will return to thee,
Ev'n sated with Varietie.

TO LUCASTA, GOING TO THE WARS

Tell me not (Sweet) I am unkinde,
   That from the Nunnerie
Of thy chaste breast, and quiet minde,
   To Warre and Armes I flie.

True; a new Mistresse now I chase,
   The first Foe in the field;
And with a stronger Faith imbrace
   A Sword, a Horse, a Shield.

Yet this inconstancy is such,
   As you too shall adore;
I could not love thee (Deare) so much,
   Lov'd I not Honour more.

ANDREW MARVELL

1621–1679

THE MOWER TO THE GLO-WORMS

Ye living Lamps, by whose dear light
The Nightingale does sit so late,
And studying all the Summer-night,
Her matchless Songs does meditate;

Ye Country Comets, that portend
No War, nor Princes funeral
Shining unto no higher end
Than to presage the Grasses fall;

Ye Glo-worms, whose officious Flame
To wandering Mowers shows the way,
That in the Night have lost their aim,
And after foolish Fires do stray;

Your courteous Lights in vain you wast,
Since Juliana here is come,
For She my Mind hath so displac'd
That I shall never find my home.

THE FAIR SINGER

To make a final conquest of all me,
Love did compose so sweet an Enemy,
In whom both Beauties to my death agree,
Joining themselves in fatal Harmony;
That while she with her Eyes my Heart does bind,
She with her Voice might captivate my Mind.

I could have fled from One but singly fair:
My dis-entangled Soul it self might save,
Breaking the curled trammels of her hair.
But how should I avoid to be her Slave,
Whose subtile Art invisibly can wreath
My Fetters of the very Air I breath?

It had been easie fighting in some plain,
Where Victory might hang in equal choice,
But all resistance against her is vain,
Who has th'advantage both of Eyes and Voice,
And all my Forces needs must be undone,
She having gained both the Wind and Sun.

Had we but World enough, and Time
This coyness, Lady, were no crime,
We would sit down, and think which way
To walk, and pass our long Loves Day.
Thou by the Indian Ganges side
Should'st Rubies find: I by the Tide
Of Humber would complain. I would
Love you ten years before the Flood:
And you should, if you please, refuse
Till the Conversion of the Jews.
My vegetable Love should grow
Vaster than Empires, and more slow.
An hundred years should go to praise
Thine Eyes, and on thy Forehead gaze.
Two hundred to adore each Breast:
But thirty thousand to the rest.
An Age at least to every part,
And the last Age should show your Heart.
For, Lady, you deserve this State;
Nor would I love at lower rate.

But at my back I always hear
Times winged Charriot hurrying near:
And yonder all before us lye
Deserts of vast Eternity.
Thy Beauty shall no more be found;
Nor, in thy marble Vault, shall sound
My echoing Song: then Worms shall try
That long preserv'd Virginity:
And your quaint Honour turn to dust;
And into ashes all my Lust.
The Grave's a fine and private place,
But none, I think, do there embrace.

Now therefore, while the youthful hew
Sits on thy skin like morning dew,
And while thy willing Soul transpires
At every pore with instant Fires,

Now let us sport us while we may;
And now, like am'rous birds of prey,
Rather at once our Time devour,
Than languish in his slow-chapt pow'r.
Let us roll all our Strength, and all
Our Sweetness, up into one Ball:
And tear our Pleasures with rough strife,
Thorough the Iron gates of Life.
Thus, though we cannot make our Sun
Stand still, yet we will make him run.

HENRY VAUGHAN

1622–1695

TO AMORET

Nimble sigh, on thy warm wings,
  Take this message and depart;
Tell Amoret, that smiles and sings,
At what thy airy voyage brings,
  That thou cam'st lately from my heart.

Tell my lovely foe that I
  Have no more such spies to send,
  But one or two that I intend,
Some few minutes ere I die,
  To her white bosom to commend.

Then whisper by that holy spring,
  Where for her sake I would have died,
Whilst those water-nymphs did bring
  Flowers to cure what she had tried;
And of my faith and love did sing.

That if my Amoret, if she
   In after-times would have it read,
How her beauty murder'd me,
With all my heart I will agree,
   If she'll but love me, being dead.

MARGARET, DUCHESS OF NEWCASTLE

1624–1674

Love, how thou'rt tired out with rhyme!
Thou art a tree whereon all poets climb;
And from thy branches every one takes some
Of thy sweet fruit, which Fancy feeds upon.
But now thy tree is left so bare and poor,
That they can hardly gather one plum more.

*

O do not grieve, Dear Heart, nor shed a tear,
Since in your eyes my life doth all appear;
And in your buried countenance my death I find;
I'm buried in your melancholy mind.

But in your smiles, I'm glorified to rise,
And your pure love doth me eternalize:
Thus by your favour you a god me make,
When in your hate a devil's shape I take.

SONG

Fool, take up thy shaft again;
$\qquad$ If thy store
Thou profusely spend in vain,
$\quad$ Who can furnish thee with more?
Throw not then away thy darts
On impenetrable hearts.

Think not thy pale flame can warm
$\qquad$ Into tears,
Or dissolve the snowy charm
$\quad$ Which her frozen bosom wears,
That expos'd, unmelted lies
To the bright suns of her eyes.

But since thou thy power hast lost,
$\qquad$ Nor canst fire
Kindle in that breast, whose frost
$\quad$ Doth these flames in mine inspire,
Not to thee but her I'll sue,
That disdains both me and you.

TWO RURAL SISTERS

Alice is tall and upright as a pine,
White as blanch'd almonds, or the falling snow,
Sweet as the damask roses when they blow,
And doubtless fruitful as the swelling vine.
Ripe to be cut, and ready to be press'd,
Her full cheek'd beauties very well appear,
And a year's fruit she loses ev'ry year,
Wanting a man to improve her to the best.

Full fain she would be husbanded, and yet,
Alas! she cannot a fit Lab'rer get
To cultivate her to her own content:
Fain would she be (God wot) about her task,
And yet (forsooth) she is too proud to ask,
And (which is worse) too modest to consent.

Marg'ret of humbler stature by the head
Is (as it oft falls out with yellow hair)
Than her fair sister, yet so much more fair,
As her pure white is better mixt with red.
This, hotter than the other ten to one,
Longs to be put into her mother's trade,
And loud proclaims she lives too long a maid,
Wishing for one t'untie her virgin zone.

She finds virginity a kind of ware,
That's very very troublesome to bear,
And being gone, she thinks will ne'er be mist:

And yet withal, the girl has so much grace,
To call for help I know she wants the face,
Though ask'd, I know not how she would resist.

JOHN DRYDEN

1631–1700

Farwell ungratfull Traytor,
  Farwell my perjur'd Swain,
Let never injur'd Creature
  Believe a Man again.
The Pleasure of Possessing
Surpasses all Expressing,
But 'tis too short a Blessing,
  And Love too long a Pain.

'Tis easie to deceive us
  In Pity of your Pain,
But when we love you leave us
  To rail at you in vain.
Before we have descry'd it,
There is no Bliss beside it,
But she that once has try'd it
  Will never love again.

The Passion you pretended
  Was only to obtain,
But when the Charm is ended
  The Charmer you disdain.
Your Love by ours we measure
Till we have lost our Treasure,
But dying is a Pleasure,
  When Living is a Pain.

ON HIS MISTRESS DROWN'D

Sweet Stream, that dost with equal Pace
Both thyself fly, and thyself chace,
 Forbear awhile to flow,
 And listen to my Woe.
Then go, and tell the Sea that all its Brine
 Is fresh compar'd to mine;
Inform it that the gentler Dame,
Who was the Life of all my Flame,
 In th'Glory of her Bud
 Has pass'd the fatal Flood,
Death by this only Stroke triumphs above
 The greatest Power of Love:
 Alas, alas! I must give o'er,
My sighs will let me add no more.
 Go on, sweet Stream, and henceforth rest
No more than does my troubled Breast;
And if my sad Complaints have made thee stay,
 These Tears, these Tears shall mend thy Way.

THOMAS FLATMAN
1637–1688

AN APPEAL TO CATS IN THE BUSINESS
OF LOVE

Ye cats that at midnight spit love at each other,
Who best feel the pangs of a passionate lover,
I appeal to your scratches and your tattered fur,
If the business of Love be no more than to purr.
Old Lady Grimalkin with her gooseberry eyes,
Knew something when a kitten, for why she is wise;
You find by experience, the love-fit's soon o'er,
Puss! Puss! lasts not long, but turns to *Cat-whore!*
    Men ride many miles,
    Cats tread many tiles,
  Both hazard their necks in the fray;
    Only cats, when they fall
    From a house or a wall,
Keep their feet, mount their tails, and away!

THE BACHELOR'S SONG

How happy a thing were a wedding
    And a bedding,
If a man might purchase a wife
  For a twelvemonth and a day;
But to live with her all a man's life,
  For ever and for ay,
Till she grow as grey as a cat,
Good faith, Mr. Parson, I thank you for that.

CYNTHIA ON HORSEBACK

Fair Cynthia mounted on her sprightly pad,
Which in white robe with silver fringe was clad,
   And swift as wind his graceful steps did move,
   As with his beauteous guide he'd been in love.
Though fierce, yet humble still to her command,
Obeying ev'ry touch of her fair hand;
   Her golden bit his foaming mouth did check,
   It spread his crest, and rais'd his bending neck.

She was the rose upon this hill of snow,
Her sparkling beauty made this glorious show;
   Whence secret flames men in their bosoms took:
The Graces and the Cupids her surround,
Attending her, while cruel she does wound,
   With switch her horse, and hearts with ev'ry look.

DESCRIBES THE PLACE WHERE CYNTHIA IS
SPORTING HERSELF

Behold yon hill, how it is swell'd with pride,
And that aspiring oak upon its side,
With how much scorn they overlook the plain,
Proud of the lovely guest they entertain.

See with what haste those crystal springs do flow
T'incorporate with the silver brook below;
There does my wanton Cynthia sporting stand,
Printing her footsteps on the yielding sand.

Look Thyrsis, how she fills with joy the place,
She bathes her feet, and views her angel's face;
Sure I've a rival of that amorous hill,
And those are streams of tears which thence distil.

INVITES HIS NYMPH TO HIS COTTAGE

On yon hill's top which this sweet plain commands,
Fair Cynthia, all alone my cottage stands,
'Gainst storms, and scorching heats well fortified,
With pines, and spreading oaks on ev'ry side.

My lovely garden too adjoining lies,
Of sweetest flowers, and of the richest dyes:
The tulip, jas'min, emony, and rose,
Of which we'll garlands for thy head compose.

Nature to make my fountain, did its part,
Which ever flows without the help of Art,
A faithful mirror shall its water be,
Where thou may'st sit beneath a shady tree.

Admiring what above the World I prize
Thyself, the object of thine own fair eyes;
And which is greatest let the Spring proclaim,
Thy powers of love, or this my amorous flame.

ON A FAIR BEGGAR

Barefoot and ragged, with neglected hair,
She whom the Heavens at once made poor and fair,
With humble voice and moving words did stay,
To beg an alms of all who pass'd that way.

But thousands viewing her became her prize,
Willingly yielding to her conquering eyes,
   And caught by her bright hairs, whilst careless she
   Makes them pay homage to her poverty.

So mean a boon, said I, what can extort
From this fair mouth, where wanton Love to sport
   Amidst the pearls and rubies we behold?
Nature on thee has all her treasures spread,
Do but incline thy rich and precious head,
   And those fair locks shall pour down showers of gold.

ON LYDIA DISTRACTED

With hairs, which for the wind to play with, hung,
   With her torn garments, and with naked feet,
   Fair Lydia dancing went from street to street,
Singing with pleasant voice her foolish song.
On her she drew all eyes in ev'ry place,
   And them to pity by her pranks did move,
   Which turn'd with gazing longer into Love
By the rare beauty of her charming face.

In all her frenzies, and her mimicries,
While she did Nature's richest gifts despise,
   There active Love did subt'ly play his part.
Her antic postures made her look more gay,
Her ragged clothes her treasures did display,
   And with each motion she ensnar'd a heart.

CHARLES SACKVILLE, EARL OF DORSET

1638–1706

SONG, WRITTEN AT SEA, IN THE FIRST DUTCH WAR, 1665, THE NIGHT BEFORE AN ENGAGEMENT

To all you Ladies now at Land,
  We Men, at Sea, indite;
But first wou'd have you understand,
  How hard it is to write;
The Muses now, and Neptune too,
We implore to write to you,
  With a Fa, la, la, la, la.

For tho' the Muses should prove kind,
  And fill our empty Brain;
Yet if rough Neptune rouze the wind,
  To wave the azure Main,
Our Paper, Pen, and Ink, and we,
Roll up and down our Ships at Sea,
  With a Fa, la, la, la, la.

Then if we write not by each Post,
  Think not we are unkind;
Nor yet conclude our Ships are lost,
  By Dutchmen, or by Wind:
Our Tears we'll send a speedier Way,
The Tide shall bring 'em twice a-day,
  With a Fa, la, la, la, la.

Let Wind and Weather do its worst,
  Be you to us but kind;
Let Dutchmen vapour, Spaniards curse,
  No sorrow we shall find:

'Tis then no matter how Things go,
Or who's our Friend, or who's our Foe,
   With a Fa, la, la, la, la.

When any mournful Tune you hear,
   That dies in ev'ry Note;
As if it sigh'd with each Man's Care,
   For being so remote;
Think then how often Love we've made
To you, when all those Tunes were play'd,
   With a Fa, la, la, la, la.

SIR CHARLES SEDLEY

1639–1701

SONG

Phillis is my only joy,
   Faithless as the winds or seas;
Sometimes coming, sometimes coy,
   Yet she never fails to please.
     If with a frown
     I am cast down,
     Phillis smiling
     And beguiling,
Makes me happier than before!

Though, alas, too late I find
   Nothing can her fancy fix,
Yet the moment she is kind,
   I forgive her all her tricks.

Which, though I see,
I can't get free;
She deceiving,
I believing;
What need lovers wish for more?

SONG

Hears not my Phillis how the birds
  Their feathered mates salute!
They tell their Passion in their words;
  Must I alone be mute?
    Phillis, without frown or smile,
    Sat and knotted all the while!

The God of Love, in thy bright eyes,
  Does like a tyrant reign!
But in thy heart, a child he lies,
  Without his dart, or flame!
    Phillis, without frown or smile,
    Sat and knotted all the while!

So many months, in silence past,
  (And yet in raging love)
Might well deserve One Word, at last,
  My Passion should approve!
    Phillis, without frown or smile,
    Sat and knotted all the while!

Must then, your faithful Swain expire?
  And not one look obtain?
Which he, to sooth his fond Desire,
  Might pleasingly explain!
    Phillis, without frown or smile,
    Sat and knotted all the while!

THE DEFIANCE

By Heaven 'tis false, I am not vain;
   And rather would the subject be
Of your indifference, or disdain,
   Than wit or raillery.

Take back the trifling praise you give,
   And pass it on some other fool,
Who may the injuring wit believe,
   That turns her into ridicule.

Tell her, she's witty, fair, and gay,
   With all the charms that can subdue:
Perhaps she'll credit what you say;
   But curse me if I do.

If your diversion you design,
   On my good-nature you have prest:
Or if you do intend it mine,
   You have mistook the jest.

A SONG

Absent from thee I languish still;
  Then ask me not, When I return?
The straying Fool 'twill plainly kill,
  To wish all Day, all Night to mourn.

Dear; from thine Arms then let me flie,
  That my fantastick Mind may prove,
The Torments it deserves to try,
  That tears my fixt Heart from my Love.

Then wearied with a world of Woe,
  To thy safe Bosom I retire,
Where Love and Peace and Truth does flow,
  May I contented there expire.

Lest once more wandering from that Heav'n,
  I fall on some base Heart unblest;
Faithless to thee, false, unforgiven,
  And lose my everlasting Rest.

THE FALL

How blest was the Created State
  Of Man and Woman e're they fell,
Compar'd to our unhappy Fate;
  We need not fear another Hell!

Naked, beneath cool Shades, they lay,
    Enjoyment waited on Desire:
Each member did their Wills obey,
    Nor could a Wish set Pleasure higher.

But we, poor Slaves to Hope and Fear,
    Are never of our Joys secure:
They lessen still as they draw near,
    And none but dull Delights endure.

Then, Chloris, while I Duty pay
    The Nobler Tribute of my Heart,
Be not You so severe to say,
    You love me for a frailer Part.

LOVE AND LIFE

All my past Life is mine no more,
    The flying Hours are gone:
Like transitory Dreams giv'n o'er,
Whose Images are kept in store,
    By Memory alone.

The Time that is to come is not;
    How can it then be mine?
The present Moment's all my Lot;
And that, as fast as it is got,
    Phillis, is only thine.

Then talk not of Inconstancy,
    False Hearts, and broken Vows;
If I, by Miracle, can be
This live-long Minute true to thee,
    'Tis all that Heav'n allows.

UPON HIS LEAVING HIS MISTRESS

'Tis not that I am weary grown
Of being yours, and yours alone:
But with what Face can I incline,
To damn you to be only mine?
You, whom some kinder Pow'r did fashion,
By Merit, and by Inclination,
The Joy at least of a whole Nation.

Let meaner Spirits of your Sex,
With humble Aims their Thoughts perplex:
And boast if by their Arts they can
Contrive to make *one* happy Man,
While, mov'd by an impartial Sense,
Favours, like Nature, you dispence,
With universal Influence.

See the kind Seed-receiving Earth,
To every Grain affords a Birth:
On her no Show'rs unwelcome fall,
Her willing Womb retains 'em all.
And shall my Caelia be confin'd?
No, live up to thy mighty Mind;
And be the Mistress of Mankind.

ANNE, COUNTESS OF WINCHILSEA

1661–1720

A LETTER TO DAPHNIS

This to the crown and blessing of my life,
The much loved husband of a happy wife;
To him whose constant passion found the art

To win a stubborn and ungrateful heart,
And to the world by tenderest proof discovers
They err, who say that husbands can't be lovers.
With such return of passion as is due,
Daphnis I love, Daphnis my thoughts pursue;
Daphnis my hopes and joys are bounded all in you.
Even I, for Daphnis' and my promise' sake,
What I in women censure, undertake.
But this from love, not vanity, proceeds;
You know who writes, and I who 'tis that reads.
Judge not my passion by my want of skill:
Many love well, though they express it ill;
And I your censure could with pleasure bear,
Would you but soon return, and speak it here.

April 2nd, 1685

MATTHEW PRIOR

1664–1721

AN ODE

The merchant, to secure his treasure,
   Conveys it in a borrow'd name:
Euphelia serves to grace my measure;
   But Cloe is my real flame.

My softest verse, my darling lyre,
   Upon Euphelia's toilet lay;
When Cloe noted her desire,
   That I should sing, that I should play.

My lyre I tune, my voice I raise;
  But with my numbers mix my sighs:
And whilst I sing Euphelia's praise,
  I fix my soul on Cloe's eyes.

Fair Cloe blush'd: Euphelia frown'd:
  I sung and gaz'd: I play'd and trembled:
And Venus to the Loves around
  Remark'd, how ill we all dissembled.

PHILLIS'S AGE

How old may Phillis be, you ask,
  Whose beauty thus all hearts engages?
To answer is no easy task:
  For she has really two ages.

Stiff in brocade, and pinch'd in stays,
  Her patches, paint, and jewels on;
All day let envy view her face,
  And Phillis is but twenty-one.

Paint, patches, jewels laid aside,
  At night astronomers agree,
The evening has the day belied;
  And Phillis is some forty-three.

NONPAREIL

Let others from the town retire,
  And in the fields seek new delight;
My Phillis does such joys inspire,
  No other objects please my sight.

In her alone I find whate'er
  Beauties a country landscape grace:
No shades so lovely as her hair,
  No plain so sweet as is her face.

Lilies and roses there combine,
  More beauteous than the flowery field;
Transparent is her skin so fine,
  To this each crystal stream must yield.

Her voice more sweet than warbling sound,
  Though sung by nightingale or lark;
Her eyes such lustre dart around,
  Compar'd to them, the sun is dark.

Both light and vital heat they give;
  Cherish'd by them, my love takes root;
From her kind looks does life receive,
  Grows a fair plant, bears flowers and fruit.

JONATHAN SWIFT

1667–1745

STELLA'S BIRTH-DAY

Stella this day is thirty-four,
(We shan't dispute a year or more:)
However, Stella, be not troubled,
Although thy size and years are doubled
Since first I saw thee at sixteen,
The brightest virgin on the green;
So little is thy form declined;

Made up so largely in thy mind.
  O, would it please the gods to split
Thy beauty, size, and years, and wit!
No age could furnish out a pair
Of nymphs so graceful, wise, and fair;
With half the lustre of your eyes,
With half your wit, your years, and size.
And then, before it grew too late,
How should I beg of gentle fate,
(That either nymph might have her swain,)
To split my worship too in twain.

WILLIAM CONGREVE

1670–1729

SONG

False though she be to me and Love,
  I'll ne'er pursue Revenge;
For still the Charmer I approve,
  Tho' I deplore her change.

In hours of Bliss we oft have met,
  They could not always last;
And though the present I regret,
  I'm grateful for the past.

THE HAPPY SWAIN

Have ye seen the morning sky,
When the dawn prevails on high,
When, anon, some purply ray
Gives a sample of the day,
When, anon, the lark, on wing,
Strives to soar, and strains to sing?

Have ye seen th'ethereal blue
Gently shedding silvery dew,
Spangling o'er the silent green,
While the nightingale, unseen,
To the moon and stars, full bright,
Lonesome chants the hymn of night?

Have ye seen the broid'red May
All her scented bloom display,
Breezes opening, every hour,
This, and that, expecting flower,
While the mingling birds prolong,
From each bush, the vernal song?

Have ye seen the damask-rose
Her unsully'd blush disclose,
Or the lilly's dewy bell,
In her glossy white, excell,
Or a garden vary'd o'er
With a thousand glories more?

By the beauties these display,
Morning, evening, night, or day
By the pleasures these excite,
Endless sources of delight!
Judge, by them, the joys I find,
Since my Rosalind was kind,
Since she did herself resign
To my vows, for ever mine.

ESTHER JOHNSON
1681–1728

TO DR. SWIFT ON HIS BIRTHDAY,
30th NOVEMBER 1721

St. Patrick's Dean, your country's pride,
My early and my only guide,
You taught how I might youth prolong,
By knowing what was right and wrong;
How from my heart to bring supplies
Of lustre to my fading eyes;
How soon a beauteous mind repairs
The loss of changed or falling hairs;
How wit and virtue from within
Send out a smoothness o'er the skin:
Your lectures could my fancy fix,
And I can please at thirty-six.
The sight of Chloe at fifteen,
Coquetting, gives me not the spleen;
The idol now of every fool
Till time shall make their passions cool;
Then tumbling down Time's steepy hill,
While Stella holds her station still.

DAMON AND CUPID

The sun was now withdrawn,
    The shepherds home were sped;
The moon wide o'er the lawn
    Her silver mantle spread;
When Damon stay'd behind,
    And saunter'd in the grove.
Will ne'er a nymph be kind,
    And give me love for love?

Oh! those were golden hours,
    When Love, devoid of cares,
In all Arcadia's bow'rs
    Lodg'd swains and nymphs by pairs!
But now from wood and plain
    Flys ev'ry sprightly lass,
No joys for me remain,
    In shades, or on the grass.

The winged boy draws near,
    And thus the swain reproves.
While beauty revell'd here,
    My game lay in the groves;
At Court I never fail
    To scatter round my arrows,
Men fall as thick as hail;
    And maidens love like sparrows.

Then, swain, if me you need,
    Strait lay your sheep-hook down;
Throw by your oaten reed,
    And haste away to town.

'O Polly, you might have toy'd and kist.
By keeping men off, you keep them on.'
 'But he so teaz'd me,
 And he so pleas'd me,
What I did, you must have done.'

*

Were I laid on Greenland's coast,
 And in my arms embrac'd my lass;
Warm amidst eternal frost,
Too soon the half year's night would pass.
Were I sold on Indian soil,
 Soon as the burning day was clos'd,
I could mock the sultry toil
 When on my charmer's breast repos'd.
And I would love you all the day,
Every night would kiss and play,
If with me you'd fondly stray
Over the hills and far away.

*

If the heart of a man is deprest with cares,
The mist is dispell'd when a woman appears;
Like the notes of a fiddle, she sweetly, sweetly
Raises the spirits, and charms our ears.
 Roses and lilies her cheeks disclose,
 But her ripe lips are more sweet than those.
  Press her,
  Caress her,
  With blisses,
  Her kisses
 Dissolve us in pleasure, and soft repose.

*

I'm like a skiff on the Ocean tost,
    Now high, now low, with each billow born,
With her rudder broke, and her anchor lost,
    Deserted and all forlorn.
While thus I lie rolling and tossing all night,
That Polly lyes sporting on seas of delight!
    Revenge, revenge, revenge,
Shall appease my restless sprite.

*

She who hath felt a real pain
    By Cupid's dart,
Finds that all absence is in vain
    To cure her heart.
Though from my lover cast
    Far as from Pole to Pole,
Still the pure flame must last,
    For love is of the Soul.

ALEXANDER POPE

1688–1744

TO MRS. M.B. ON HER BIRTH-DAY

Oh be thou blest with all that Heav'n can send,
Long Health, long Youth, long Pleasure, and a Friend;
Not with those Toys the female world admire,
Riches that vex, and Vanities that tire.
Not as the world its pretty Slaves rewards,
A Youth of Frolicks, an Old-Age of Cards;
Fair to no Purpose, artful to no End;

Young without Lovers, old without a Friend;
A Fop their Passion, but their Prize a Sot;
Alive, ridiculous; and dead, forgot!
　　Let Joy or Ease, let Affluence or Content,
And the gay Conscience of a life well spent,
Calm ev'ry thought, inspirit ev'ry Grace,
Glow in thy heart, and smile upon thy face.
Let day improve on day, and year on year,
Without a Pain, a Trouble, or a Fear;
Till Death unfelt that tender frame destroy,
In some soft Dream, or Extasy of joy:
Peaceful sleep out the Sabbath of the Tomb,
And wake to Raptures in a Life to come.

PHILIP DORMER STANHOPE, EARL OF CHESTERFIELD

1694–1773

TO MISS ELEANOR AMBROSE ON THE OCCA-SION OF HER WEARING AN ORANGE LILY AT A BALL IN DUBLIN CASTLE ON JULY THE 12TH

Say, lovely Tory, why the Jest,
Of wearing Orange on thy Breast,
When that same Breast betraying shows
The whiteness of the rebel Rose?

SONG

One day the god of fond desire,
  On mischief bent, to Damon said,
'Why not disclose your tender fire?
  Not own it to the lovely maid?'

The shepherd marked his treacherous art,
  And, softly sighing, thus replied:
' 'Tis true, you have subdued my heart,
  But shall not triumph o'er my pride.

'The slave in private only bears
  Your bondage, who his love conceals;
But when his passion he declares,
  You drag him at your chariot-wheels.'

HINT FROM VOITURE

Let Sol his annual journeys run,
And when the radiant task is done,
Confess, through all the globe, 'twould pose him
To match the charms that Celia shows him.

And should he boast he once had seen
As just a form, as bright a mien,
Yet must it still for ever pose him
To match—what Celia never shows him.

William Collins

1721–1759

SONNET

When Phoebe form'd a wanton smile,
  My soul! it reach'd not here!
Strange that thy peace, thou trembler, flies
  Before a rising tear!

From midst the drops, my love is born,
  That o'er those eyelids rove:
Thus issued from a teeming wave
  The fabled queen of love.

Christopher Smart

1722–1771

SONG

Where shall Celia fly for shelter,
  In what secret grove or cave?
Sighs and sonnets sent to melt her

From the young, the gay, the brave,
Tho' with prudish airs she starch her,
    Still she longs, and still she burns;
Cupid shoots like Hayman's archer,
Wheresoe'r the damsel turns.

Virtue, wit, good sense, and beauty,
    If discretion guide us not,
Sometimes are the ruffian's booty,
    Sometimes are the booby's lot:
Now they're purchas'd by the trader,
    Now commanded by the peer;
Now some subtle mean invader
    Wins the heart, or gains the ear.

O discretion, thou'rt a jewel,
    Or our grandmammas mistake;
Stinting flame by baiting fewel,
    Always careful and awake!
Wou'd you keep your pearls from tramplers,
    Weigh the license, weigh the banns:
Mark my song upon your samplers,
    Wear it on your knots and fans.

WILLIAM COWPER

1731–1800

TO MARY

The twentieth year is well-nigh past,
Since first our sky was overcast;
Ah would that this might be the last!
                            My Mary!

Thy spirits have a fainter flow,
I see thee daily weaker grow—
'Twas my distress that brought thee low,
                    My Mary!

Thy needles, once a shining store,
For my sake restless heretofore,
Now rust disus'd, and shine no more,
                    My Mary!

For though thou gladly wouldst fulfil
The same kind office for me still,
Thy sight now seconds not thy will,
                    My Mary!

But well thou play'dst the housewife's part,
And all thy threads with magic art
Have wound themselves about this heart,
                    My Mary!

Thy indistinct expressions seem
Like language utter'd in a dream;
Yet me they charm, whate'er the theme,
                    My Mary!

Thy silver locks, once auburn bright,
Are still more lovely in my sight
Than golden beams of orient light,
                    My Mary!

For could I view nor them nor thee,
What sight worth seeing could I see?
The sun would rise in vain for me,
                    My Mary!

Partakers of thy sad decline,
Thy hands their little force resign;
Yet, gently prest, press gently mine,
                    My Mary!

And then I feel that still I hold
A richer store ten thousandfold
Than misers fancy in their gold,
    My Mary!

Such feebleness of limbs thou prov'st,
That now at every step thou mov'st
Upheld by two; yet still thou lov'st,
    My Mary!

And still to love, though prest with ill,
In wintry age to feel no chill,
With me is to be lovely still,
    My Mary!

But ah! by constant heed I know.
How oft the sadness that I show
Transforms thy smiles to looks of woe,
    My Mary!

And should my future lot be cast
With much resemblance of the past,
Thy worn-out heart will break at last,
    My Mary!

THOMAS CHATTERTON

1752–1770

MYNSTRELLES SONGE

O! synge untoe mie roundelaie,
O! droppe the brynie teare wythe mee,
Daunce ne moe atte hallie daie,
Lycke a reynynge ryver bee;

Mie love ys dedde,
Gon to hys deathe-bedde,
Al under the wyllowe tree.

Blacke hys cryne as the wyntere nyghte,
Whyte hys rode as the sommer snowe,
Rodde hys face as the mornynge lyghte,
Cale he lyes the grave belowe;
    Mie love is dedde,
    Gon to hys deathe-bedde,
    Al under the wyllow tree.

Swote hys tyngue as the throstles note,
Quycke ynn daunce as thoughte canne bee,
Defte hys taboure, codgelle stote,
O! hee lyes bie the wyllowe tree:
    Mie love ys dedde,
    Gon to hys deathe-bedde,
    Al under the wyllowe tree.

Harke! the ravenne flappes hys wynge,
In the briered delle belowe;
Harke! the dethe-owle loude dothe synge,
To the nyghte-mares as heie goe;
    Mie love ys dedde,
  Gon to hys deathe-bedde,
    Al under the wyllowe tree.

See! the whyte moone sheenes onne hie;
Whyterre ys mie true loves shroude;
Whyterre yanne the mornynge skie,
Whyterre yanne the evenynge cloude;
    Mie love ys dedde,
    Gon to hys death-bedde,
    Al under the wyllowe tree.

Heere, uponne mie true loves grave,
Schalle the baren fleurs be layde,
Nee one hallie Seynete to save
Al the celness of a mayde.
    Mie love ys dedde,
      Gon to hys deathe-bedde,
      Alle under the wyllow tree.

Wythe mie hondes I'lle dente the brieres
Rounde his hallie corse to gre,
Ouphante fairie, lyghte youre fyres,
Heere mie boddie stylle schalle bee.
    Mie love ys dedde,
      Gon to hys deathe-bedde,
      All under the wyllowe tree.

Comme, wythe acorne-coppe and thorne,
Drayne mie hartys blodde awaie;
Lyfe and all yttes goode I scorne,
Daunce bie nete, or feaste bie daie.
    Mie love ys dedde,
      Gon to hys deathe-bedde,
      Al under the wyllowe tree.

Waterre wytches, crownede wythe reytes,
Bere mee to yer leathalle tyde.
I die; I comme; mie true love waytes.
Thos the damselle spake and dyed.

dente = fasten	cryne = hair
reytes = waterflags	rode = complexion
celness = coldness	

MYNSTRELLES SONGE

Angelles bee wrogte to bee of neidher kynde;
Angelles alleyne fromme chafe desyre bee free;
Dheere ys a somwhatte evere yn the mynde,

Yatte, wythout wommanne, cannot stylled bee,
Ne seyncte yn celles, botte, havynge blodde and tere,
Do fynde the spryte to joie on syghte of womanne fayre:

Wommen bee made, notte for hemselves botte manne,
Bone of hys bone, and chyld of hys desire;
Fromme an ynutylle membere fyrste beganne,
Ywroghte with moche of water, lyttele fyre;
Therefore theie seke the fyre of love, to hete
The milkyness of kynde, and make hemselfes complete.

Albeytte, wythout wommen, menne were pheeres
To salvage kynde, and wulde botte lyve to slea,
Botte wommenne efte the spryghte of peace so cheres,
Tochelod yn Angel joie heie Angeles bee;
Go, take thee swythyn to thie bedde a wyfe,
Bee bante or blejsed hie yn proovynge marryage lyfe.

pheeres = equal		tochelod = joined
efte = often		swythyn = quickly
	bante = cursed	

GEORGE CRABBE

1754–1832

The ring, so worn as you behold,
So thin, so pale, is yet of gold.
The passion such it was to prove:
Worn with life's care, love yet was love.

SONG

How sweet I roam'd from field to field,
    And tasted all the summer's pride,
Till I the prince of love beheld,
    Who in the sunny beams did glide!

He shew'd me lilies for my hair,
    And blushing roses for my brow;
He led me through his gardens fair,
    Where all his golden pleasures grow.

With sweet May dews my wings were wet,
    And Phoebus fir'd my vocal rage;
He caught me in his silken net,
    And shut me in his golden cage.

He loves to sit and hear me sing,
    Then, laughing, sports and plays with me;
Then stretches out my golden wing,
    And mocks my loss of liberty.

THE CLOD AND THE PEBBLE

'Love seeketh not Itself to please,
Nor for itself hath any care,
But for another gives its ease,
And builds a Heaven in Hell's despair.'

So sang a little Clod of Clay
Trodden with the cattle's feet,
But a Pebble of the brook
Warbled out these metres meet:

'Love seeketh only Self to please,
To bind another to Its delight,
Joys in another's loss of ease,
And builds a Hell in Heaven's despite.'

THE SICK ROSE

O rose, thou art sick!
The invisible worm
That flies in the night,
In the howling storm,

Has found out thy bed
Of crimson joy,
And his dark secret love
Does thy life destroy.

THE GARDEN OF LOVE

I went to the Garden of Love,
And saw what I never had seen:
A Chapel was built in the midst,
Where I used to play on the green.

And the gates of the Chapel were shut,
And 'Thou shalt not' writ over the door;
So I turn'd to the Garden of Love
That so many sweet flowers bore;

And I saw it was filled with graves,
And tomb-stones where flowers should be;
And Priests in black gowns were walking their rounds,
And binding with briars my joys and desires.

*

Never seek to tell thy love
Love that never told can be;
For the gentle wind does move
Silently, invisibly.

I told my love, I told my love,
I told her all my heart,
Trembling, cold, in ghastly fears—
Ah, she did depart.

Soon as she was gone from me
A traveller came by
Silently, invisibly;
O, was no deny.

*

I laid me down upon a bank
Where love lay sleeping.
I heard among rushes dank
Weeping, Weeping.

Then I went to the heath and the wild
To the thistles and thorns of the waste
And they told me how they were beguil'd,
Driven out, and compel'd to be chaste.

A slumber did my spirit seal;
  I had no human fears;
She seemed a thing that could not feel
  The touch of earthly years.

No motion has she now, no force;
  She neither hears nor sees;
Rolled round in earth's diurnal course,
  With rocks, and stones, and trees.

*

She dwelt among the untrodden ways
  Beside the springs of Dove,
A Maid whom there were none to praise
  And very few to love:

A violet by a mossy stone
  Half hidden from the eye!
Fair as a star, when only one
  Is shining in the sky.

She lived unknown, and few could know
  When Lucy ceased to be;
But she is in her grave, and, oh,
  The difference to me!

SONG

'A weary lot is thine, fair maid,
  A weary lot is thine!
To pull the thorn thy brow to braid,
  And press the rue for wine!
A lightsome eye, a soldier's mien,
  A feather of the blue,
A doublet of the Lincoln green,—
  No more of me you knew,
                    My Love!
  No more of me you knew.

This morn is merry June, I trow,
  The rose is budding fain;
But we shall bloom in winter snow,
  Ere we two meet again,'
He turned his charger as he spake,
  Upon the river shore,
He gave his bridle-reins a shake,
  Said, 'Adieu for evermore,
                    My Love!
  And adieu for evermore.'

THE JILTED NYMPH

I'm jilted, forsaken, outwitted;
   Yet think not I'll whimper or brawl—
The lass is alone to be pitied
   Who ne'er has been courted at all:
Never by great or small,
Woo'd or jilted at all;
   Oh, how unhappy's the lass
Who has never been courted at all!

What though at my heart he has tilted,
   What though I have met with a fall?
Better be courted and jilted
   Than never be courted at all.
Woo'd and jilted and all,
Still I will dance at the ball;
   And waltz and quadrille
   With light heart and heel,
With proper young men and tall.

Past ruin'd Ilion Helen lives,
   Alcestis rises from the shades;
Verse calls them forth; 'tis verse that gives
   Immortal youth to mortal maids.

Soon shall Oblivion's deepening veil
  Hide all the peopled hills you see,
The gay, the proud, while lovers hail
  These many summers you and me.

*

Proud word you never spoke, but you will speak
  Four not exempt from pride some future day.
Resting on one white hand a warm wet cheek
  Over my open volume you will say,
  'This man loved *me!*' then rise and trip away.

*

Ah, what avails the sceptred race!
  Ah, what the form divine!
What every virtue, every grace!
  Rose Aylmer, all were thine.

Rose Aylmer, whom these wakeful eyes
  May weep, but never see,
A night of memories and of sighs
  I consecrate to thee.

*

Mild is the parting year, and sweet
  The odour of the falling spray;
Life passes on more rudely fleet,
  And balmhess is its closing day.

I wait its close, I court its gloom,
  But mourn that never must there fall
Or on my breast or on my tomb
  The tear that would have soothed it all.

*

When Helen first saw wrinkles in her face
('Twas when some fifty long had settled there
And intermarried and brancht off awide)
She threw herself upon her couch, and wept:
On this side hung her head, and over that
Listlessly she let fall the faithless brass
That made the men so faithless.

                              But when you
Found them, or fancied them, and would not hear
That they were only vestiges of smiles,
Or the impression of some amorous hair
Astray from cloistered curls and roseat band,
Which had been lying there all night perhaps
Upon a skin so soft . . . *No, no*, you said,
Sure, they are coming, yes, are come, are here . . .
Well, and what matters it . . . while you are too!

                     *

Ye walls! sole witnesses of happy sighs,
   Say not, blest walls, one word,
Remember, but keep safe from ears and eyes
   All you have seen and heard.

THOMAS MOORE

1779–1852

SONG

Where is the nymph, whose azure eye
   Can shine through rapture's tear!
The sun has sunk, the moon is high,
   And yet she comes not here!

Was that her footstep on the hill—
　　Her voice upon the gale?—
No, 'twas the wind, and all is still,
　　Oh, maid of Marlivale!

Come to me, love, I've wander'd far,
　　'Tis past the promis'd hour;
Come to me, love, the twilight star
　　Shall guide thee to my bower.

THE KISS

Give me, my love, that billing kiss
　　I taught you one delicious night,
When, turning epicures in bliss,
　　We tried inventions of delight.

Come, gently steal my lips along,
　　And let your lips in murmurs move,—
Ah, no!—again—that kiss was wrong—
　　How can you be so dull, my love?

'Cease, cease!' the blushing girl replied—
　　And in her milky arms she caught me—
'How can you thus your pupil chide;
　　You know *'twas in the dark* you taught me!'

AN ARGUMENT

I've oft been told by learned friars,
　　That wishing and the crime are one,
And Heaven punishes desires
　　As much as if the deed were done.

If wishing damns us, you and I
   Are damn'd to all our heart's content;
Come, then, at least we may enjoy
   Some pleasure for our punishment!

TO . . .

When I loved you, I can't but allow
   I had many an exquisite minute;
But the scorn that I feel for you now
   Hath even more luxury in it!

Thus, whether we're on or we're off,
   Some witchery seems to await you;
To love you is pleasant enough,
   But oh! 'tis delicious to hate you!

QUANTUM EST QUOD DESIT

'Twas a new feeling—something more
Than we had dar'd to own before,
   Which then we hid not;
We saw it in each other's eye,
And wish'd in every broken sigh
   To speak, but did not!

She felt my lips' impassion'd touch;
'Twas the first time I dar'd so much,
   And yet, she chid not;
But whisper'd o'er my burning brow,
'Oh! do you doubt I love you now?'
   Sweet soul! I did not!

Warmly I felt her bosom thrill,
I prest it closer, closer still,
  Though gently bid not;
Till—oh! the world hath seldom heard
Of lovers, who so nearly err'd,
  And yet who—did not!

GEORGE GORDON, LORD BYRON

1788–1824

SONG

So, we'll go no more a-roving
  So late into the night,
Though the heart be still as loving,
  And the moon be still as bright.

For the sword outwears its sheath,
  And the soul wears out the breast,
And the heart must pause to breathe,
  And love itself have rest.

Though the night was made for loving,
  And the day returns too soon,
Yet we'll go no more a-roving
  By the light of the moon.

ON A CALM SUMMER'S NIGHT

The night is calm, the cygnet's down
  Scarce skims the lake along;
The throstle to the hazel's flown,
  To trill his evening song.

The curling woodbine now appears
  More sweet than fragrant gems;
The sky a robe of crimson wears,
  The scale-clad beetle hums.

What pleasure, walking with my Jane,
  Earth's truest, best delight,
Returning to embrace again,
  And loath to say good night.

TO STELLA
From the Greek of Plato

Thou wert the morning star among the living,
  Ere thy fair light had fled;—
Now, having died, thou art as Hesperus, giving
  New splendour to the dead.

A HATE-SONG

A Hater he came and sat by a ditch,
  And he took an old cracked lute;
And he sang a song which was more of a screech
  'Gainst a woman that was a brute.

JOHN CLARE

1793–1864

MARY

It is the evening hour,
  How silent all doth lie:
The hornèd moon she shows her face
  In the river with the sky.
Prest by the path on which we pass,
The flaggy lake lies still as glass.

Spirit of her I love,
  Whispering to me
Stories of sweet visions as I rove,
  Here stop, and crop with me
Sweet flowers that in the still hour grew—
We'll take them home, nor shake off the bright dew.

Mary, or sweet spirit of thee,
  As the bright sun shines to-morrow
Thy dark eyes these flowers shall see,
  Gathered by me in sorrow,
Into the still hour when my mind was free
To walk alone—yet wish I walked with thee.

FIRST LOVE

I ne'er was struck before that hour
   With love so sudden and so sweet.
Her face it bloomed like a sweet flower
   And stole my heart away complete.
My face turned pale as deadly pale,
   My legs refused to walk away,
And when she looked 'what could I ail?'
   My life and all seemed turned to clay.

And then my blood rushed to my face
   And took my sight away.
The trees and bushes round the place
   Seemed midnight at noonday.
I could not see a single thing,
   Words from my eyes did start;
They spoke as chords do from the string
   And blood burnt round my heart.

Are flowers the winter's choice?
   Is love's bed always snow?
She seemed to hear my silent voice
   And love's appeal to know.
I never saw so sweet a face
   As that I stood before:
My heart has left its dwelling-place
   And can return no more.

STANZAS

Black absence hides upon the past,
   I quite forgot thy face;
And memory like the angry blast
   Will love's last smile erase.

RUTH

She stood breast high amid the corn,
Clasp'd by the golden light of morn,
Like the sweetheart of the sun,
Who many a glowing kiss had won.

On her cheek an autumn flush,
Deeply ripened;—such a blush
In the midst of brown was born,
Like red poppies grown with corn.

Round her eyes her tresses fell,
Which were blackest none could tell,
But long lashes veil'd a light
That had else been all too bright.

And her hat, with shady brim,
Made her tressy forehead dim;
Thus she stood amid the stooks,
Praising God with sweetest looks:

Sure, I said, heav'n did not mean,
Where I reap thou shouldst but glean,
Lay thy sheaf adown and come,
Share my harvest and my home.

With you first shown to me,
With you first known to me,
My life-time loom'd, in hope, a length of joy:
Your voice so sweetly spoke,
Your mind so meetly spoke,
My hopes were all of bliss without alloy,
As I, for your abode, sought out, with pride,
This house with vines o'er-ranging all its side.

I thought of years to come,
All free of tears to come,
When I might call you mine, and mine alone,
With steps to fall for me,
And day cares all for me,
And hands for ever nigh to help my own;
And then thank'd Him who had not cast my time
Too early or too late for your sweet prime.

Then bright was dawn, o'er dew,
And day withdrawn, o'er dew,
And mid-day glow'd on flow'rs along the ledge,
And wall in sight, afar,
Were shining white, afar,
And brightly shone the stream beside the sedge.
But still, the fairest light of those clear days
Seem'd that which fell along your flow'ry ways.

THE WIFE A-LOST

Since I noo mwore do zee your feäce,
   Up steärs or down below,
I'll zit me in the lwonesome pleäce,
   Where flat-bough'd beech do grow:
Below the beeches' bough, my love,
   Where you did never come,
An' I don't look to meet ye now,
   As I do look at hwome.

Since you noo mwore be at my zide,
   In walks in zummer het,
I'll goo alwone where mist do ride,
   Drough trees a-drippen wet:
Below the raïn-wet bough, my love,
   Where you did never come,
An' I don't grieve to miss ye now,
   As I do grieve at hwome.

Since now bezide my dinner-bwoard
   Your vaïce do never sound,
I'll eat the bit I can avword,
   A-vield upon the ground;
Below the darksome bough, my love,
   Where you did never dine,
An' I don't grieve to miss ye now,
   As I at hwome do pine.

Since I do miss your vaïce an' feäce
   In präyer at eventide,
I'll praÿ wi oone sad vaïce vor greäce
   To goo where you do bide;
Above the tree an' bough, my love,
   Where you be gone avore,
An' be a-waïten vor me now,
   To come vor evermwore.

JUNE BRACKEN AND HEATHER
To ——

There on the top of the down,
The wild heather round me and over me June's high blue,
When I look'd at the bracken so bright and the heather so brown,
I thought to myself I would offer this book to you,
This and my love together,
To you that are seventy-seven,
With a faith as clear as the heights of the June-blue heaven,
And a fancy as summer-new
As the green of the bracken amid the gloom of the heather.

THE DAISY
Written at Edinburgh

O love, what hours were thine and mine,
In lands of palm and southern pine;
  In lands of palm, of orange-blossom,
Of olive, aloe, and maize and vine.

Nor knew we well what pleased us most,
Not the clipt palm of which they boast;
  But distant colour, happy hamlet,
A moulder'd citadel on the coast,

Or tower, or high hill-convent, seen
A light amid its olives green;
  Or olive-hoary cape in ocean;
Or rosy blossom in hot ravine.

What more? we took our last adieu,
And up the snowy Splugen drew,
  But ere we reach'd the highest summit
I pluck'd a daisy, I gave it you.

It told of England then to me,
And now it tells of Italy.
  O love, we two shall go no longer
To lands of summer across the sea;

So dear a life your arms enfold
Whose crying is a cry for gold:
  Yet here to-night in this dark city,
When ill and weary, alone and cold,

I found, tho' crush'd to hard and dry,
This nursling of another sky
  Still in the little book you lent me,
And where you tenderly laid it by:

And I forgot the clouded Forth,
The gloom that saddens Heaven and Earth
  The bitter east, the misty summer
And gray metropolis of the North.

Perchance, to lull the throbs of pain,
Perchance, to charm a vacant brain,
  Perchance, to dream you still beside me,
My fancy fled to the South again.

THE COURTSHIP OF THE YONGHY-BONGHY-BO

On the Coast of Coromandel
  Where the early pumpkins blow,
    In the middle of the woods
    Lived the Yonghy-Bonghy-Bo.
Two old chairs, and half a candle,—
One old jug without a handle,—
    These were all his worldly goods:
    In the middle of the woods,
    These were all the worldly goods
  Of the Yonghy-Bonghy-Bo,
  Of the Yonghy-Bonghy-Bo.

Once among the Bong-trees walking
  Where the early pumpkins blow,
    To a little heap of stones
    Came the Yonghy-Bonghy-Bo.
There he heard a Lady talking
To some milk-white hens of Dorking,—
    ' 'Tis the Lady Jingly Jones!
    On that little heap of stones
    Sits the Lady Jingly Jones!'
  Said the Yonghy-Bonghy-Bo.
  Said the Yonghy-Bonghy-Bo.

'Lady Jingly! Lady Jingly!
  Sitting where the pumpkins blow,
    Will you come and be my wife?'
  Said the Yonghy-Bonghy-Bo.
'I am tired of living singly,—

On this coast so wild and shingly,—
     I'm a-weary of my life;
     If you'll come and be my wife,
     Quite serene would be my life!'—
   Said the Yonghy-Bonghy-Bo,
   Said the Yonghy-Bonghy-Bo.

'On this Coast of Coromandel,
   Shrimps and watercresses grow,
     Prawns are plentiful and cheap,'
   Said the Yonghy-Bonghy-Bo.
'You shall have my chairs and candle,
And my jug without a handle!—
     Gaze upon the Rolling deep
     (Fish is plentiful and cheap);
     As the sea, my love is deep!'
   Said the Yonghy-Bonghy-Bo.
   Said the Yonghy-Bonghy-Bo.

Lady Jingly answered sadly,
   And her tears began to flow,—
     'Your proposal comes too late,
   Mr. Yonghy-Bonghy-Bo!
I would be your wife most gladly!'
(Here she twirled her fingers madly)
     'But in England I'v⁻ a mate!
     Yes! you've asked me far too late,
     For in England I've a mate,
   Mr. Yonghy-Bonghy-Bo!
   Mr Yonghy-Bonghy-Bo!

'Mr. Jones—(his name is Handel,—
   Handel Jones, Esquire, & Co.)
     Dorking fowls delights to send,—
   Mr. Yonghy-Bonghy-Bo!
Keep, oh! keep your chairs and candle,—
And your jug without a handle,—

127

I can merely be your friend!
—Should my Jones more Dorkings send,
I will give you three, my friend!
Mr. Yonghy-Bonghy-Bo!
Mr. Yonghy-Bonghy-Bo!

'Though you've such a tiny body,
    And your head so large doth grow,—
        Though your hat may blow away,
    Mr. Yonghy-Bonghy-Bo!
Though you're such a Hoddy Doddy—
Yet I wish that I could modi-
        fy the words I needs must say!
        Will you please to go away?
        That is all I have to say—
    Mr. Yonghy-Bonghy-Bo!
    Mr. Yonghy-Bonghy-Bo!'

Down the slippery slopes of Myrtle,
    Where the early pumpkins blow,
        To the calm and silent sea
    Fled the Yonghy-Bonghy-Bo.
There, beyond the Bay of Gurtle,
Lay a large and lively Turtle;—
        'You're the Cove', he said, 'for me;
        On your back beyond the sea,
        Turtle, you shall carry me!'
    Said the Yonghy-Bonghy-Bo.
    Said the Yonghy-Bonghy-Bo.

Through the silent-roaring ocean
    Did the Turtle swiftly go;
        Holding fast upon his shell
    Rode the Yonghy-Bonghy-Bo.
With a sad primaeval motion
Towards the sunset isles of Boshen
        Still the Turtle bore him well.

Holding fast upon his shell,
'Lady Jingly Jones, farewell!'
Sang the Yonghy-Bonghy-Bo.
Sang the Yonghy-Bonghy-Bo.

From the Coast of Coromandel,
    Did the Lady never go;
        On the heap of stones she mourns
    For the Yonghy-Bonghy-Bo.
On the Coast of Coromandel,
In his jug without a handle,
        Still she weeps, and daily moans;
        On that little heap of stones
        To her Dorking Hens she moans,
    For the Yonghy-Bonghy-Bo.
    For the Yonghy-Bonghy-Bo.

ROBERT BROWNING

1812–1889

NEVER THE TIME AND THE PLACE

Never the time and the place
    And the loved one all together!
This path—how soft to pace!
    This May—what magic weather!
Where is the loved one's face?
In a dream that loved one's face meets mine,
    But the house is narrow, the place is bleak
Where, outside, rain and wind combine
    With a furtive ear, if I strive to speak,
    With hostile eye at my flushing cheek,

With a malice that marks each word, each sign!
O enemy sly and serpentine,
   Uncoil thee from the waking man!
     Do I hold the Past
     Thus firm and fast
   Yet doubt if the Future hold I can?
This path so soft to pace shall lead
Thro' the magic of May to herself indeed!·
Or narrow if needs the house must be,
Outside are the storms and strangers: we—
Oh, close, safe, warm sleep I and she,
—I and she!

RESPECTABILITY

Dear, had the world in its caprice
   Deigned to proclaim 'I know you both,
Have recognized your plighted troth,
   Am sponsor for you: live in peace!'—
How many precious months and years
   Of youth had passed, that speed so fast,
Before we found it out at last,
   The world, and what it fears?

How much of priceless life were spent
   With men that every virtue decks,
And women models of their sex
   Society's true ornament,—
Ere we dared wander, nights like this,
   Through wind and rain, and watch the Seine,
And feel the Boulevart break again
   To warmth and light and bliss?

I know! the world proscribes not love;
   Allows my finger to caress
Your lip's contour and downiness,
   Provided it supply a glove.

The world's good word!—the Institute!
  Guizot receives Montalembert!
Eh? Down the court three lampions flare:
  Put forward your best foot!

LOVE

So, the year's done with!
  (*Love me for ever!*)
All March begun with,
  April's endeavour;
May-wreaths that bound me
  June needs must sever;
Now snows fall round me,
  Quenching June's fever—
  (*Love me for ever!*)

THOMAS BURBIDGE

1816–1895

SHE BEWITCHED ME

She bewitched me
With such a sweet and genial charm,
I knew not when I wounded was,
And when I found it, hugged the harm.

Down hill; ah yes—down hill, down hill I glide,
But such a hill!
One tapestried fall of meadow pride,
Of ladysmock and daffodil.

How soon, how soon adown a rocky stair,
And slips no longer smooth as they are sweet,
Shall I, with backward-streaming hair,
Outfly my bleeding feet?

REMEMBRANCE

Cold in the earth, and the deep snow piled above thee!
Far, far removed, cold in the dreary grave!
Have I forgot, my Only Love, to love thee,
Severed at last by Time's all-severing wave?

Now, when alone, do my thoughts no longer hover
Over the mountains, on that northern shore,
Resting their wings where heath and fern-leaves cover
Thy noble heart for ever, ever more?

Cold in the earth, and fifteen wild Decembers
From those brown hills have melted into spring:
Faithful indeed is the spirit that remembers
After such years of change and suffering!

Sweet Love of youth, forgive if I forget thee
While the World's tide is bearing me along:
Sterner desires and darker hopes beset me,
Hopes which obscure, but cannot do thee wrong!

No later light has lightened up my heaven,
No second morn has ever shone for me;
All my life's bliss from thy dear life was given,
All my life's bliss is in the grave with thee.

But when the days of golden dreams had perished
And even Despair was powerless to destroy,
Then did I learn how existence could be cherished,
Strengthened and fed without the aid of joy.

Then did I check the tears of useless passion,
Weaned my young soul from yearning after thine;
Sternly denied its burning wish to hasten
Down to that tomb already more than mine.

And even yet, I dare not let it languish,
Dare not indulge in memory's rapturous pain;
Once drinking deep of that divinest anguish,
How could I seek the empty world again?

*

Come, the wind may never again
Blow as now it blows for us;
And the stars may never again shine as now they shine;
Long before October returns,
Seas of blood will have parted us;
And you must crush the love in your heart, and I the love
     in mine!

*

If grief for grief can touch thee,
If answering woe for woe,
If any ruth can melt thee,
Come to me now!

I cannot be more lonely,
More drear I cannot be!
My worn heart throbs so wildly
'Twill break for thee.

And when the world despises,
When heaven repels my prayer,
Will not mine angel comfort?
Mine idol hear?

Yes, by the tears I've poured thee,
By all my hours of pain,
O I shall surely win thee,
Beloved, again!

THOMAS CAULFIELD IRWIN

1823–1892

IPHIONE

Where in the summer-warm woodlands with the sweet wind,
  From yon blue ocean, solitarily smiling,
    Wanderest thou, with tresses
    Cinctureless, in wildernesses
Of whispering leaves and blown foam, like a fleet hind,
  With virginal phantasies the hours beguiling?—
    Now the cool, curved waves chasing,
    Or, bosom-billowed, embracing
Cold passionless lovers of the eternal sea,
  Throbbing with broken breathings innumerably:
    Or, couched, with wet ear listening
    To what some wreathed shell glistening
With dry salt sprays and rainbow colours is telling—
Close to thy airy soul of its measureless dwelling—
    Melodies of the sad brine,
    Remote and lonely, dim, divine.

WITH THE DAWN

Husband

Why have you risen, to stand with naked feet
And thin robe stirring in the airs of night,
Looking from the casement?

Wife

It is sweet
To view upon the broad sea, glimmering white,
Sails, in the low moonlight.

Husband

I dream'd that you were lost to me afar,
And I had just recovered you once more.
Why linger you?—

Wife

To watch that last large star
Sparkle our cradled child's calm slumber o'er.
Soft as the little wave that sweet and frore
Rises and sinks upon the sandy shore,—
   He breathes; and on his face there comes a smile,
   Just as the dawn's pale gold has touched, the while,
Yon faint cloud cradled on the distant deep.
   The calm sea-level turns from white to rose;
   And, as the space a richer glory grows,
The earliest bird sings faintly far away
   Upon the poplar by the ocean steep.

Husband

Awake him not, oh, dear one, till 'tis day;
   To be alive, and suffer not, is sleep.

THE KISS

'I saw you take his kiss!' ' 'Tis true.'
  'O, modesty!' ' 'Twas strictly kept:
He thought me asleep; at least I knew
  He thought I thought he thought I slept.'

A FAREWELL

With all my will, but much against my heart,
We two now part.
My Very Dear,
Our solace is, the sad road lies so clear.
It needs no art,
With faint, averted feet
And many a tear,
In our opposed paths to persevere.
Go thou to East, I West.
We will not say
There's any hope, it is so far away.
But, O, my Best,
When the one darling of our widowhead,
The nursling Grief,
Is dead,
And no dews blur our eyes
To see the peach-bloom come in evening skies,
Perchance we may,
Where now this night is day,
And even through faith of still averted feet,

Making full circle of our banishment,
Amazed meet;
The bitter journey to the bourne so sweet
Seasoning the termless feast of our content
With tears of recognition never dry.

A WARNING

I saw, and trembled for the day
When you should see her beauty, gay
And pure as apple-blooms, that show
Outside a blush and inside snow,
Her high and touching elegance
Of order'd life as free as chance.
Ah, haste from her bewitching side,
No friend for you, far less a bride!
He that but once too nearly hears
The music of forefended spheres,
Is thenceforth lonely, and for all
His days like one who treads the Wall
Of China, and, on this hand, sees
Cities and their civilities,
And, on the other, lions.

LOVE SERVICEABLE

What measure Fate to him shall mete
    Is not the noble Lover's care;
He's heart-sick with a longing sweet
    To make her happy as she's fair.
Oh, misery, should she him refuse,
    And so her dearest good mistake!
His own success he thus pursues
    With frantic zeal for her sole sake.

To lose her were his life to blight,
  Being loss to hers; to make her his,
Except as helping her delight,
  He calls but incidental bliss;
And, holding life as so much pelf
  To buy her posies, learns this lore:
He does not rightly love himself
  Who does not love another more.

THE STORM

Within the pale blue haze above,
  Some pitchy shreds took size and form,
And, like a madman's wrath or love,
  From nothing rose a sudden storm.
The blossom'd limes, which seem'd to exhale
  Her breath, were swept with one strong sweep,
And up the dusty road the hail
  Came like a flock of hasty sheep,
Driving me under a cottage-porch,
  Whence I could see the distant spire,
Which, in the darkness, seem'd a torch
  Touch'd with the sun's retreating fire.
A voice, so sweet that even her voice,
  I thought, could scarcely be more sweet,
As thus I stay'd against my choice,
  Did mine attracted hearing greet;
And presently I turn'd my head
  Where the kind music seem'd to be,
And where, to an old blind man, she read
  The words that teach the blind to see.
She did not mark me; swift I went,
  Thro' the fierce shower's whistle and smoke,
To her home, and thence her woman sent
  Back with umbrella, shoes, and cloak.

The storm soon pass'd; the sun's quick glare
    Lay quench'd in vapour fleecy, fray'd;
And all the moist, delicious air
    Was fill'd with shine that cast no shade;
And, when she came, forth the sun gleam'd,
    And clash'd the trembling Minster chimes;
And the breath with which she thank'd me seem'd
    Brought thither from the blossom'd limes.

THE REVELATION

An idle poet, here and there,
    Looks round him; but, for all the rest,
The world, unfathomably fair,
    Is duller than a witling's jest.
Love wakes men, once a lifetime each;
    They lift their heavy lids, and look;
And, lo, what one sweet page can teach
    They read with joy, then shut the book.
And some give thanks, and some blaspheme,
    And most forget; but, either way,
That and the Child's unheeded dream
Is all the light of all their day.

THE ROSY BOSOM'D HOURS

A florin to the willing Guard
    Secured, for half the way,
(He lock'd us in, ah, lucky-starr'd)
    A curtain'd, front coupé.
The sparkling sun of August shone;
    The wind was in the West;
Your gown and all that you had on
    Was what became you best;

No sacred bard did e'er invent
  With such wild wit as placed,
Betwixt Love's either continent,
  The isthmus of your waist;
Or rounded fine each little breast,
  And set so fair apart,
As if to cradle Love's unrest
  Upon your very heart;
And we were in that seldom mood
  When soul with soul agrees,
Mingling, like flood with equal flood,
  In agitated ease.
Far round, each blade of harvest bare
  Its little load of bread;
Each furlong of that journey fair
  With separate sweetness sped.
The calm of use was coming o'er
  The wonder of our wealth
And now, maybe, 'twas not much more
  Than Eden's common health.
We pace the sunny platform, while
  The train at Havant changed:
What made the people kindly smile,
  Or stare with looks estranged?
Too radiant for a wife you seem'd,
  Serener than a bride;
Me happiest born of men I deem'd,
  And show'd perchance my pride.
I loved that girl, so gaunt and tall,
  Who whispered loud, 'Sweet Thing!'
Scanning your figure, slight yet all
  Round as your own gold ring.
At Salisbury you stray'd alone
  Within the shafted glooms,
Whilst I was by the Verger shown
  The brasses and the tombs.
At tea we talk'd of matters deep,
  Of joy that never dies;

140

We laugh'd, till love was mix'd with sleep
    Within your great sweet eyes.
The next day, sweet with luck no less
    And sense of sweetness past,
The full tide of our happiness
    Rose higher than the last.
At Dawlish, 'mid the pools of brine,
    You swept from rock to rock,
One hand quick tightening upon mine,
    One holding up your frock.
On starfish and on weeds alone
    You seem'd intent to be:
Flash'd those great gleams of hope unknown
    From you, or from the sea?
Ne'er came before, ah, when again
    Shall come two days like these:
Such quick delight within the brain,
    Within the heart such peace?
I thought, indeed, by magic chance,
But as, at dusk, we reach'd Penzance,
    A drizzling rain set in.

WILLIAM ALLINGHAM

1824–1889

AN EVENING

A sunset's mounded cloud;
    A diamond evening-star;
    Sad blue hills afar;
    Love in his shroud.

Scarcely a tear to shed;
  Hardly a word to say;
  The end of a summer day;
    Sweet Love dead.

SONG

I walk'd in the lonesome evening,
  And who so sad as I,
When I saw the young men and maidens
  Merrily passing by.
    To thee, my Love, to thee—
    So fain would I come to thee!
While the ripples fold upon sands of gold
    And I look across the sea.

I stretch out my hands; who will clasp them?
  I call,—thou repliest no word:
O why should heart-longing be weaker
  Than the waving wings of a bird!
    To thee, my Love, to thee—
    So fain would I come to thee!
For the tide's at rest from east to west,
    And I look across the sea.

There's joy in the hopeful morning,
  There's peace in the parting day,
There's sorrow with every lover
  Whose true love is far away.
    To thee, my Love, to thee—
    So fain would I come to thee!
And the water's bright in a still moonlight,
    As I look across the sea.

THE ORCHARD-PIT

Piled deep below the screening apple-branch
  They lie with bitter apples in their hands:
And some are only ancient bones that blanch,
And some had ships that last year's wind did launch,
  And some were yesterday the lords of lands.

In the soft dell, among the apple-trees,
  High up above the hidden pit she stands,
And there for ever sings, who gave to these,
That lie below, her magic hour of ease,
  And those her apples holden in their hands.

This in my dreams is shown me; and her hair
  Crosses my lips and draws my burning breath;
Her song spreads golden wings upon the air,
Life's eyes are gleaming from her forehead fair,
  And from her breasts the ravishing eyes of Death.

Men say to me that sleep hath many dreams,
  Yet I knew never but this dream alone:
There, from a dried-up channel, once the stream's,
The glen slopes up; even such in sleep it seems
  As to my waking sight the place well known.

My love I call her, and she loves me well:
  But I love her as in the maelstrom's cup
The whirled stone loves the leaf inseparable
That clings to it round all the circling swell,
  And that the same last eddy swallows up.

GEORGE MEREDITH

1828–1909

MODERN LOVE

i

By this he knew she wept with waking eyes:
That, at his hand's light quiver by her head,
The strange low sobs that shook their common bed
Were called into her with a sharp surprise,
And strangled mute, like little gasping snakes,
Dreadfully venomous to him. She lay
Stone-still, and the long darkness flowed away
With muffled pulses. Then, as midnight makes
Her giant heart of Memory and Tears
Drink the pale drug of silence, and so beat
Sleep's heavy measure, they from head to feet
Were moveless, looking through their dead black years,
By vain regret scrawled over the blank wall.
Like sculptured effigies they might be seen
Upon their marriage-tomb, the sword between;
Each wishing for the sword that severs all.

xliii

Mark where the pressing wind shoots javelin-like
Its skeleton shadow on the broad-backed wave!
Here is a fitting spot to dig Love's grave;
Here where the ponderous breakers plunge and strike,
And dart their hissing tongues high up the sand:
In hearing of the ocean, and in sight
Of those ribbed wind-streaks running into white.
If I the death of Love had deeply planned,
I never could have made it half so sure,
As by the unblest kisses which upbraid

The full-waked sense; or failing that, degrade!
'Tis morning: but no morning can restore
What we have forfeited. I see no sin:
The wrong is mixed. In tragic life, God wot,
No villain need be! Passions spin the plot:
We are betrayed by what is false within.

xlvii

We saw the swallows gathering in the sky,
And in the osier-isle we heard them noise.
We had not to look back on summer joys,
Or forward to a summer of bright dye:
But in the largeness of the evening earth
Our spirits grew as we went side by side.
The hour became her husband and my bride.
Love, that had robbed us so, thus blessed our dearth!
The pilgrims of the year waxed very loud
In multitudinous chatterings, as the flood
Full brown came from the West, and like pale blood
Expanded to the upper crimson cloud.
Love, that had robbed us of immortal things,
This little moment mercifully gave;
Where I have seen across the twilight wave
The swan sail with her young beneath her wings.

l

Thus piteously Love closed what he begat:
The union of this ever-diverse pair!
These two were rapid falcons in a snare,
Condemned to do the flitting of the bat.
Lovers beneath the singing sky of May,
They wandered once; clear as the dew on flowers:
But they fed not on the advancing hours:
Their hearts held cravings for the buried day.
Then each applied to each that fatal knife,
Deep questioning, which probes to endless dole.
Ah, what a dusty answer gets the soul

When hot for certainties in this our life!—
In tragic hints here see what evermore
Moves dark as yonder midnight ocean's force,
Thundering like ramping hosts of warrior horse,
To throw that faint thin line upon the shore!

CHRISTINA ROSSETTI

1830–1894

REMEMBER

Remember me when I am gone away,
Gone far away into the silent land;
When you can no more hold me by the hand,
Nor I half turn to go yet turning stay.
Remember me when no more day by day
You tell me of our future that you plann'd:
Only remember me; you understand
It will be late to counsel then or pray.
Yet if you should forget me for a while
And afterwards remember, do not grieve:
For if the darkness and corruption leave
A vestige of the thoughts that once I had,
Better by far you should forget and smile
Than that you should remember and be sad.

FROM THE ANTIQUE

The wind shall lull us yet,
    The flowers shall spring above us:
And those who hate forget,
    And those forget who love us.

The pulse of hope shall cease,
   Of joy and of regretting:
We twain shall sleep in peace,
   Forgotten and forgetting.

For us no sun shall rise,
   Nor wind rejoice, nor river,
Where we with fast-closed eyes
   Shall sleep and sleep for ever.

JOHN LEICESTER WARREN, LORD DE TABLEY

1835–1895

A SONG OF DUST

When we, my love, are gone to dust,
   And nature, as of old, is fair:
When on thy rosy cheek is rust,
   And stain sepulchral on thy hair;

When from the slab, that marks our sleep,
   The raindrop eats our names away:
And cushioned lichens gently creep
   To make the beaming letters gray;

These tears, I weep upon thy hand,
   Shall pass as leaves in autumn air,
And who unborn shall understand,
   If thou wert sweet, if thou wert fair?

Who shall explain this lovely thing
   To generations yet to be?

Will evanescent beauty wing
  Her flight to dim futurity?

No lease is hers of lengthened hours:
  Her love, a momentary ray,
Crisping the calyx of the flowers,
  Is sped before the lift of day.

A little while the whitethorn blows,
  And all the grasses rarely spring.
Then crimsons out the wild field rose,
  And swallows rest their travelled wing.

And fair are maidens in their prime;
  And lovers pledge eternal truth,
When for an hour the cup of Time
  Is nectar on the lips of youth.

Love and the nest of birds are sweet;
  Till, like a broken hope, the flower,
Warm at the early sunbeam's feet,
  Lies shattered cold at evening's hour.

The ages in an endless tide
  Advance their still encroaching feet:
The present, like a golden bride,
  Is faultless for an hour and sweet.

Time will not stay for thee, my love,
  The clouds are coming and the snow;
The thunder rocks the realms above—
  One farewell kiss before we go.

FAREWELL TO JULIET

I see you, Juliet, still, with your straw hat
Loaded with vines, and with your dear pale face,
On which those thirty years so lightly sat,
And the white outline of your muslin dress.
You wore a little *fichu* trimmed with lace
And crossed in front, as was the fashion then,
Bound at your waist with a broad band or sash,
All white and fresh and virginally plain.
There was a sound of shouting far away
Down in the valley, as they called to us,
And you, with hands clasped seeming still to pray
Patience of fate, stood listening to me thus
With heaving bosom. There a rose lay curled.
It was the reddest rose in all the world.

ST. VALENTINE'S DAY

To-day, all day, I rode upon the down,
With hounds and horsemen, a brave company.
On this side in its glory lay the sea,
On that the Sussex weald, a sea of brown.
The wind was light, and brightly the sun shone,
And still we galloped on from gorse to gorse.
And once, when checked, a thrush sang, and my horse
Pricked his quick ears as to a sound unknown.
I knew the Spring was come. I knew it even
Better than all by this, that through my chase

In bush and stone and hill and sea and heaven
I seemed to see and follow still your face.
Your face my quarry was. For it I rode,
My horse a thing of wings, myself a god.

THOMAS HARDY

1840–1928

AFTER A JOURNEY

Hereto I come to view a voiceless ghost;
   Whither, O whither will its whim now draw me?
Up the cliff, down, till I'm lonely, lost,
   And the unseen waters' ejaculations awe me.
Where you will next be there's no knowing,
   Facing round about me everywhere,
     With your nut-coloured hair,
And gray eyes, and rose-flush coming and going.

Yes: I have re-entered your olden haunts at last;
   Through the years, through the dead scenes I have tracked
     you;
What have you now found to say of our past—
   Scanned across the dark space wherein I have lacked you?
Summer gave us sweets, but autumn wrought division?
   Things were not lastly as firstly well
     With us twain, you tell?
But all's closed now, despite Time's derision.

I see what you are doing: you are leading me on
   To the spots we knew when we haunted here together,
The waterfall, above which the mist-bow shone
   At the then fair hour in the then fair weather,

150

And the cave just under, with a voice still so hollow
　　That it seems to call out to me from forty years ago,
　　　　When you were all aglow,
And not the thin ghost that I now fraily follow!

Ignorant of what there is flitting here to see,
　　The waked birds preen and the seals flop lazily,
Soon you will have, Dear, to vanish from me,
　　For the stars close their shutters and the dawn whitens
　　　　hazily.
Trust me, I mind not, though Life lours,
　　The bringing me here; nay, bring me here again!
　　　　I am just the same as when
Our days were a joy, and our paths through flowers.

THE VOICE

Woman much missed, how you call to me, call to me,
Saying that now you are not as you were
When you had changed from the one who was all to me,
But as at first, when our day was fair.

Can it be you that I hear? Let me view you, then,
Standing as when I drew near to the town
Where you would wait for me: yes, as I knew you then,
Even to the original air-blue gown!

Or is it only the breeze, in its listlessness
Travelling across the wet mead to me here,
You being ever dissolved to wan wistlessness,
Heard no more again far or near?

　　　　Thus I; faltering forward,
　　　　Leaves around me falling,
Wind oozing thin through the thorn from norward,
　　　　And the woman calling.

IN A CATHEDRAL CITY

These people have not heard your name;
No loungers in this placid place
Have helped to bruit your beauty's fame.

The grey Cathedral, towards whose face
Bend eyes untold, has met not yours;
Your shade has never swept its base.

Your form has never darked its doors,
Nor have your faultless feet once thrown
A pensive pit-pat on its floors.

Along the street to maids well known
Blithe lovers hum their tender airs,
But in your praise voice not a tone . . .

—Since nought bespeaks you here, or bears,
As I, your imprint through and through,
Here might I rest, till my heart shares
The spot's unconsciousness of you!

A THUNDERSTORM IN TOWN
(*A Reminiscence:* 1893)

She wore a new 'terra-cotta' dress,
And we stayed, because of the pelting storm,
Within the hansom's dry recess,
Though the horse had stopped; yea, motionless
    We sat on, snug and warm.

Then the downpour ceased, to my sharp sad pain
And the glass that had screened our forms before
Flew up, and out she sprang to her door:
I should have kissed her if the rain
    Had lasted a minute more.

FAINTHEART IN A RAILWAY TRAIN

At nine in the morning there passed a church,
At ten there passed me by the sea,
At twelve a town of smoke and smirch,
At two a forest of oak and birch,
   And then, on a platform, she:

A radiant stranger, who saw not me.
I said, 'Get out to her do I dare?'
But I kept my seat in my search for a plea,
And the wheels moved on. O could it but be
   That I had alighted there!

Arthur O'Shaughnessy

1844–1881

Hath any loved you well, down there,
   Summer or winter through?
Down there, have you found any fair
   Laid in the grave with you?
Is death's long kiss a richer kiss
   Than mine was wont to be—
Or have you gone to some far bliss
   And quite forgotten me?

What soft enamouring of sleep
   Hath you in some soft way?
What charmed death holdeth you with deep
   Strange lure by night and day?

—A little space below the grass,
  Out of the sun and shade;
But worlds away from me, alas,
  Down there where you are laid?

Hold me no longer for a word
  I used to say or sing:
Ah, long ago you must have heard
  So many a sweeter thing:
For rich earth must have reached your heart
  And turned the faith to flowers;
And warm wind stolen, part by part,
  Your soul through faithless hours.

ANDREW LANG

1844–1912

CHANGEFUL BEAUTY
(*From the Greek*)

Whether I find thee bright with fair,
Or still as bright with raven hair;
With equal grace thy tresses shine,
Ah, queen, and Love will dwell divine
In these thy locks, on that far day,
When gold or sable turns to grey!

I will not let thee go.
Ends all our month-long love in this?
    Can it be summed up so,
    Quit in a single kiss?
I will not let thee go.

I will not let thee go.
If thy words' breath could scare thy deeds,
    As the soft south can blow
    And toss the feathered seeds,
Then might I let thee go.

I will not let thee go.
Had not the great sun seen, I might;
    Or were he reckoned slow
    To bring the false to light,
Then might I let thee go.

I will not let thee go.
The stars that crowd the summer skies
    Have watched us so below
    With all their million eyes,
I dare not let thee go.

I will not let thee go.
Have we not chid the changeful moon,
    Now rising late and now
    Because she set too soon,
And shall I let thee go?

I will not let thee go.
Have not the young flowers been content,
 Plucked ere their buds could blow,
 To seal our sacrament?
 I cannot let thee go.

I will not let thee go.
I hold thee by too many bands:
 Thou sayest farewell, and lo!
 I have thee by the hands,
 And will not let thee go.

MICHAEL FIELD

1846–1914

Ah me, if I grew sweet to man
It was but as a rose that can
No longer keep the breath that heaves
And swells among its folded leaves.

The pressing fragrance would unclose
The flower, and I become a rose,
That unimpeachable and fair
Planted its sweetness in the air.

No art I used men's love to draw;
I lived but by my being's law,
As roses are by heaven designed
To bring the honey to the wind.

JEALOUSY

'The myrtle bush grew shady
　　Down by the ford.'—
'Is it even so?' said my lady.
　　'Even so!' said my lord.
'The leaves are set too thick together
　　For the point of a sword.'

'The arras in your room hangs close,
　　No light between!
You wedded one of those
　　That see unseen."—
'Is it even so?' said the King's Majesty.
　　'Even so!' said the Queen.

NON SUM QUALIS ERAM BONAE SUB REGNO CYNARAE

Last night, ah, yesternight, betwixt her lips and mine
There fell thy shadow, Cynara! thy breath was shed
Upon my soul between the kisses and the wine;

And I was desolate and sick of an old passion,
  Yea, I was desolate and bowed my head:
I have been faithful to thee, Cynara! in my fashion.

All night upon mine heart I felt her warm heart beat,
Night-long within mine arms in love and sleep she lay;
Surely the kisses of her bought red mouth were sweet;
But I was desolate and sick of an old passion,
  When I awoke and found the dawn was gray:
I have been faithful to thee, Cynara! in my fashion.

I have forgot much, Cynara! gone with the wind,
Flung roses, roses riotously with the throng,
Dancing to put thy pale, lost lilies out of mind;
But I was desolate and sick of an old passion,
  Yea, all the time, because the dance was long:
I have been faithful to thee, Cynara! in my fashion.

I cried for madder music and for stronger wine,
But when the feast is finished and the lamps expire,
Then falls thy shadow, Cynara! the night is thine;
And I am desolate and sick of an old passion:
  Yea, hungry for the lips of my desire:
I have been faithful to thee, Cynara! in my fashion.

VICTOR PLARR

1863–1929

EPITAPHIUM CITHARISTRIAE

Stand not uttering sedately
  Trite oblivious praise above her!
Rather say you saw her lately
  Lightly kissing her last lover.

Whisper not, 'There is a reason
  Why we bring her no white blossom';
Since the snowy bloom's in season
  Strow it on her sleeping bosom:

Oh, for it would be a pity
  To o'erpraise her or to flout her:
She was wild, and sweet, and witty—
  Let's not say dull things about her.

W. B. YEATS

1865–1939

DOWN BY THE SALLEY GARDENS

Down by the salley gardens my love and I did meet;
She passed the salley gardens with little snow-white feet.
She bid me take love easy, as the leaves grow on the tree;
But I, being young and foolish, with her would not agree.

In a field by the river my love and I did stand,
And on my leaning shoulder she laid her snow-white hand.
She bid me take life easy, as the grass grows on the weirs;
But I was young and foolish, and now am full of tears.

NO SECOND TROY

Why should I blame her that she filled my days
With misery, or that she would of late
Have taught to ignorant men most violent ways,
Or hurled the little streets upon the great,

Had they but courage equal to desire?
What could have made her peaceful with a mind
That nobleness made simple as a fire,
With beauty like a tightened bow, a kind
That is not natural in an age like this,
Being high and solitary and most stern?
Why, what could she have done, being what she is?
Was there another Troy for her to Burn?

AFTER LONG SILENCE

Speech after long silence; it is right,
All other lovers being estranged or dead,
Unfriendly lamplight hid under its shade,
The curtains drawn upon unfriendly night,
That we descant and yet again descant
Upon the supreme theme of Art and Song:
Bodily decrepitude is wisdom; young
We loved each other and were ignorant.

ARTHUR SYMONS

1865–1945

IN KENSINGTON GARDENS

Under the almond tree,
Room for my love and me!
Over our heads the April blossom;
April-hearted are we.

Under the pink and white,
Love in her eyes alight;
Love and the Spring of Kensington Gardens:
Hey for the heart's delight!

LAUS VIRGINITATIS

The mirror of men's eyes delights me less,
O mirror, than the friend I find in thee;
Thou lovest, as I love, my loveliness,
Thou givest my beauty back to me.

I to myself suffice; why should I tire
The heart with roaming that would rest at home?
Myself the limit to my own desire,
I have no desire to roam.

I hear the maidens crying in the hills;
'Come up among the bleak and perilous ways,
Come up and follow after Love, who fills
The hollows of our nights and days;

'Love the deliverer, who is desolate,
And saves from desolation; the divine
Out of great suffering; Love, compassionate,
Who is thy bread and wine.

'O soul, that faints in following after him.'
I hear; but what is Love that I should tread
Hard ways among the perilous passes dim,
Who need no succouring wine and bread?

Enough it is to dream, enough to abide
Here where the loud world's echoes fall remote,
Untroubled, unawakened, satisfied;
As water-lilies float.

Lonely upon a shadow-sheltered pool,
Dreaming of their own whiteness; even so,
I dwell within a nest of shadows cool,
And watch the vague hours come and go.

They come and go, but I my own delight
Remain, and I desire no change in aught:
Might I escape indifferent Time's despite,
That ruins all he wrought!

This dainty body formed so curiously,
So delicately and wonderfully made,
My own, that none hath ever shared with me,
My own, and for myself arrayed;

All this that I have loved and not another,
My own desire's delight, this, shall Time bring
Where Beauty hath the abhorred worm for brother,
The dust for covering?

At least I bear it virgin to the grave,
Pure, and apart, and rare, and casketed;
What, living, was my own and no man's slave,
Shall be my own when I am dead.

But thou, my friend, my mirror, dost possess
The shadow of myself that smiles in thee,
And thou dost give, with thy own loveliness,
My beauty back to me.

JULIET

How did the party go in Portman Square?
I cannot tell you; Juliet was not there.
And how did Lady Gaster's party go?
Juliet was next me and I do not know.

W. H. Davies

1871–1940

THE FLIRT

A pretty game, my girl,
  To play with me so long;
Until this other lover
  Comes dancing to thy song,
And my affair is over.

But love, though well adored,
  Is not my only note:
So let thy false love-prattle
  Be in another man's throat
That weaker man's death-rattle.

Ah, such as thou, at last,
     Wilt take a false man's hand:
Think kindly then of me,
     When thou'rt forsaken, and
The shame sits on thy knee.

HER MERRIMENT

When I had met my love the twentieth time,
   She put me to confession day and night:
Did I like woman far above all things,
   Or did the songs I make give more delight?

'Listen, you sweeter flower than ever smiled
   In April's sunny face,' I said at last—
'The voices and the legs of birds and women
   Have always pleased my ears and eyes the most.'

And saying this, I watched my love with care,
   Not knowing would my words offend or please:
But laughing gaily, her delighted breasts
   Sent ripples down her body to her knees.

WALTER DE LA MARE

1873–1956

THE GHOST

'Who knocks?' 'I, who was beautiful,
   Beyond all dreams to restore,
I, from the roots of the dark thorn am hither,
   And knock on the door.'

'Who speaks?' 'I—once was my speech
   Sweet as the bird's on the air,
When echo lurks by the waters to heed;
   'Tis I speak thee fair.'

'Dark is the hour!' 'Ay, and cold.'
   'Lone is my house.' 'Ah, but mine?'
'Sight, touch, lips, eyes yearned in vain.'
   'Long dead these to thine. . . .'

Silence. Still faint on the porch
   Brake the flames of the stars.
In gloom groped a hope-wearied hand
   Over keys, bolts, and bars.

A face peered. All the grey night
   In chaos of vacancy shone;
Naught but vast sorrow was there—
   The sweet cheat gone.

MOONLIGHT

The far moon maketh lovers wise
   In her pale beauty trembling down,
Lending curved cheeks, dark lips, dark eyes,
   A strangeness not her own.
And, though they shut their lids to kiss,
   In starless darkness peace to win,
Even on that secret world from this
   Her twilight enters in.

ALONE

The abode of the nightingale is bare,
Flowered frost congeals in the gelid air,
The fox howls from his frozen lair:

Alas, my loved one is gone,
I am alone:
It is winter.

Once the pink cast a winy smell,
The wild bee hung in the hyacinth bell,
Light in effulgence of beauty fell:
     Alas, my loved one is gone,
     I am alone:
     It is winter.

My candle a silent fire doth shed,
Starry Orion hunts o'erhead;
Come moth, come shadow, the world is dead:
     Alas, my loved one is gone,
     I am alone;
     It is winter.

EDWARD THOMAS

1878–1917

LIKE THE TOUCH OF RAIN

Like the touch of rain she was
On a man's flesh and hair and eyes
When the joy of walking thus
Has taken him by surprise:

With the love of the storm he burns,
He sings, he laughs, well I know how,
But forgets when he returns
As I shall not forget her 'Go now'.

Those two words shut a door
Between me and the blessed rain
That was never shut before
And will not open again.

HAROLD MONRO

1879–1932

THE TERRIBLE DOOR

Too long outside your door I have shivered.
You open it? I will not stay.
I'm haunted by your ashen beauty.
Take back your hand. I have gone away.

Don't talk, but move to that near corner.
I loathe the long cold shadow here.
We will stand a moment in the lamplight,
Until I watch you hard and near.

Happy release! Good-bye for ever!
Here at the corner we say good-bye.
But if you want me, if you do need me,
Who waits, at the terrible door, but I?

BALLAD OF THE LONDONER

Evening falls on the smoky walls,
  And the railings drip with rain,
And I will cross the old river
  To see my girl again.

The great and solemn-gliding tram,
  Love's still-mysterious car,
Has many a light of gold and white,
  And a single dark red star.

I know a garden in a street
  Which no one ever knew;
I know a rose beyond the Thames,
  Where flowers are pale and few.

D. H. LAWRENCE

1885–1930

GLOIRE DE DIJON

When she rises in the morning
I linger to watch her;
She spreads the bath-cloth underneath the window
And the sunbeams catch her

Glistening white on the shoulders,
While down her sides the mellow
Golden shadow glows as
She stoops to the sponge, and her swung breasts
Sway like full-blown yellow
Gloire de Dijon roses.

She drips herself with water, and her shoulders
Glisten as silver, they crumple up
Like wet and falling roses, and I listen
For the sluicing of their rain-dishevelled petals.
In the window full of sunlight
Concentrates her golden shadow
Fold on fold, until it glows as
Mellow as the glory roses.

RUPERT BROOKE

1887–1915

SAFETY

Dear! of all happy in the hour, most blest
   He who has found our hid security,
Assured in the dark tides of the world that rest,
   And heard our word, 'Who is so safe as we?'
We have found safety with all things undying,
   The winds, and morning, tears of men and mirth,
The deep night, and birds singing, and clouds flying,
   And sleep, and freedom, and the autumnal earth.

We have built a house that is not for Time's throwing.
   We have gained a peace unshaken by pain for ever.
War knows no power. Safe shall be my going,

Secretly armed against all death's endeavour;
Safe though all safety's lost; safe where men fall;
And if these poor limbs die, safest of all.

IVOR GURNEY

1890–1937

THE LOVE SONG

Out of the blackthorn edges
I caught a tune
And before it could vanish, seized
It, wrote it down.

Gave to a girl, so praising
Her eyes, lips and hair
She had little knowing, it was only thorn
Had dreamed of a girl there.

Prettily she thanked me, and never
Guessed any of my deceit. . . .
But O Earth is this the only way
Man may conquer, a girl surrender her sweet.

GREATER LOVE

Red lips are not so red
   As the stained stones kissed by the English dead.
Kindness of wooed and wooer
Seems shame to their love pure.
O Love, your eyes lose lure
   When I behold eyes blinded in my stead!

Your slender attitude
   Trembles not exquisite like limbs knife-skewed,
Rolling and rolling there
Where God seems not to care;
Till the fierce Love they bear
   Cramps them in death's extreme decrepitude.

Your voice sings not so soft,—
   Though even as wind murmuring through raftered loft,—
Your dear voice is not dear,
Gentle, and evening clear,
As theirs whom none now hear,
   Now earth has stopped their piteous mouths that coughed.

Heart, you were never hot,
   Nor large, nor full like hearts made great with shot;
And though your hand be pale,
Paler are all which trail
Your cross through flame and hail:
   Weep, you may weep, for you may touch them not.

THE WINDOW SILL

Presage and caveat not only seem
To come in dream,
But do so come in dream.

When the cock crew and phantoms floated by,
This dreamer I
Out of the house went I,

Down long unsteady streets to a mad square;
And who was there,
Or whom did I know there?

Julia, leaning on her window sill.
'I love you still,'
She said, 'O love me still!'

I answered: 'Julia, do you love me best?'
'What of this breast,'
She mourned, 'this flowery breast?'

Then a wild sobbing spread from door to door,
And every floor
Cried shame on every floor,

As she unlaced her bosom to disclose
Each breast a rose,
A white and cankered rose.

A LOST JEWEL

Who on your breast pillows his head now,
Jubilant to have won
The heart beneath on fire for him alone,

At dawn will hear you, plagued by nightmare,
Mumble and weep
About some blue jewel you were sworn to keep.

Wake, blink, laugh out in reassurance,
Yet your tears will say:
'It was not mine to lose or give away.

'For love it shone—never for the madness
Of a strange bed—
Light on my finger, fortune in my head.'

Roused by your naked grief and beauty,
For lust he will burn:
'Turn to me, sweetheart! Why do you not turn?'

EDMUND BLUNDEN

1896–1974

LATE LIGHT

Come to me when the swelling wind assails the wood with a sea-
    like roar.
While the yellow west is still afire; come borne by the wind up the
    hillside track;
  There is quiet yet, and brightness more
  Than day's clear fountains to noon rayed back
    If you come;

If you will come, and against this fall
Of leaves and light and what seemed time,
Now changed to haste, against them all
Glow, calm and young; O help me climb
Above the entangling phantoms harrying
Shaken ripeness, unsighted prime;
Come unwithering and unvarying—
Tell claw-handed Decline to scrawl
A million menaces on the wall
For whom it will; while safe we two
Moved where no knife-gust ever blew,
And no boughs crack, and no bells toll,
Through the tempest's ominous interval,
   Penitential low recall.

FRANCES CORNFORD

1886–1960

TWO POEMS

I

She Warns Him

I am a lamp, a lamp that is out;
  I am a shallow stream;
In it are neither pearls or trout,
  Nor one of the things that you dream.

Why do you smile and deny, my lover?
  I will not be denied.
I am a book, a book with a cover,
  And nothing at all inside.

Here is the truth, and you must grapple,
  Grapple with what I have said.
I am a dumpling without any apple,
  I am a star that is dead.

II

All Souls' Night

My love came back to me
Under the November tree
Shelterless and dim.
He put his hand upon my shoulder,
He did not think me strange or older,
Nor I, him.

CECIL DAY LEWIS

1904–1972

THE ALBUM

I see you, a child
In a garden sheltered for buds and playtime,
Listening as if beguiled
By a fancy beyond your years and the flowering maytime.
The print is faded: soon there will be
No trace of that pose enthralling,
Nor visible echo of my voice distantly calling
'Wait! Wait for me!'

Then I turn the page
To a girl who stands like a questioning iris
By the waterside, at an age
That asks every mirror to tell what the heart's desire is.
The answer she finds in that oracle stream
Only time could affirm or disprove,
Yet I wish I was there to venture a warning, 'Love
Is not what you dream'.

Next you appear
As if garlands of wild felicity crowned you—
Courted, caressed, you wear
Like immortelles the lovers and friends around you.
'They will not last you, rain or shine,
They are but straws and shadows,'
I cry: 'Give not to those charming desperadoes
What was made to be mine.'

One picture is missing—
The last. It would show me a tree stripped bare
By intemperate gales, her amazing
Noonday of blossom spoilt which promised so fair.
Yet, scanning those scenes at your heyday taken,
I tremble, as one who must view
In the crystal a doom he could never deflect—yes, I too
Am fruitlessly shaken.

I close the book;
But the past slides out of its leaves to haunt me
And it seems, wherever I look,
Phantoms of irreclaimable happiness taunt me.
Then I see her, petalled in new-blown hours,
Beside me—'All you love most there
Has blossomed again,' she murmurs, 'all that you missed there
Has grown to be yours.'

ABOVE THE HIGH

Cold Oxford unfamiliar now, around:
Brilliance of naked April
On the Christ Church Meadow: Six a.m.
  Below my window, cold,
  All thinnest clearest purest
  Blue and shine.

Trees have not leaved
And want the rain: I know—
  Birds scream and sing, rook cawings go
  And cross, or clash: White
  Stones are whiter now they are not seen.

I am awake, awake again,
Who heard the mediaeval hours
Strike through,
And in this wide still-opening so pale blue
Of unfamiliar day, alone
In white and virgin undergraduate's room,
Alive, alive, the feeling
Enters me again which fills me full of you,
Once closer than warm adjective to noun,
Who are the one thing warm,
Objectified, and new,
  Elsewhere—*elsewhere*—inside
  This selfsame cold abstract
  So ancient town.

MADRIGAL

Your love is dead, lady, your love is dead;
Dribbles no sound
From his stopped lips, though swift underground
Spurts his wild hair.

Your love is dead, lady, your love is dead;
Faithless he lies
Deaf to your call, though shades of his eyes
Break through and stare.

WINTER

The tree still bends over the lake,
And I try to recall our love,
Our love which had a thousand leaves.

VILLANELLE

It is the pain, it is the pain, endures.
Your chemic beauty burned my muscles through.
Poise of my hands reminded me of yours.

What later purge from this deep toxin cures?
What kindness now could the old salve renew?
It is the pain, it is the pain, endures.

The infection slept (custom or change inures)
And when pain's secondary phase was due
Poise of my hands reminded me of yours.

How safe I felt, whom memory assures,
Rich that your grace safely by heart I knew.
It is the pain, it is the pain, endures.

My stare drank deep beauty that still allures.
My heart pumps yet the poison draught of you.
Poise of my hands reminded me of yours.

You are still kind whom the same shape immures.
Kind and beyond adieu. We miss our cue.
It is the pain, it is the pain, endures.
Poise of my hands reminded me of yours.

IN A BATH TEASHOP

'Let us not speak, for the love we bear one another—
    Let us hold hands and look.'
She, such a very ordinary little woman;
    He, such a thumping crook:
But both, for the moment, little lower than the angels
    In the teashop inglenook.

THE ARCHAEOLOGICAL PICNIC

In this high pasturage, the Blunden time,
With Lady's finger, Smokewort, Lovers' Loss,
And lin-lan-lone a Tennysonian chime
Stirring the sorrel and the gold-starred moss,
Cool is the chancel, bright the Altar cross.

Drink, Mary, drink your fizzy lemonade
And leave the king-cups. Take your grey felt hat;
Here, where the low-side window lends a shade,
There, where the key lies underneath the mat
The rude forefathers of the hamlet sat.

Sweet smell of cerements and cold wet stones,
Hassock and cassock, paraffin and pew,
Green in a light which that sublime Burne Jones
White-hot and wondering from the glass kiln drew
Gleams and re-gleams this Trans arcade anew.

So stand you waiting, freckled innocence!
For me the squinch and squint and Trans arcade;
For you, where meadow grass is evidence,
With flattened pattern, of our picnic made,
One bottle more of fizzy lemonade.

W. H. AUDEN

1907–1973

SONG XI

Lay your sleeping head, my love,
Human on my faithless arm;
Time and fevers burn away
Individual beauty from
Thoughtful children, and the grave
Proves the child ephemeral:
But in my arms till break of day
Let the living creature lie,
Mortal, guilty, but to me
The entirely beautiful.

Soul and body have no bounds:
To lovers as they lie upon
Her tolerant enchanted slope
In their ordinary swoon,
Grave the vision Venus sends
Of supernatural sympathy,
Universal love and hope;
While an abstract insight wakes
Among the glaciers and the rocks
The hermit's sensual ecstasy.

Certainty, fidelity
On the stroke of midnight pass
Like vibrations of a bell,
And fashionable madmen raise
Their pedantic boring cry:
Every farthing of the cost,
All the dreaded cards foretell,
Shall be paid, but from this night
Not a whisper, not a thought,
Not a kiss nor look be lost.

Beauty, midnight, vision dies:
Let the winds of dawn that blow
Softly round your dreaming head
Such a day of sweetness show
Eye and knocking heart may bless,
Find the mortal world enough;
Noons of dryness see you fed
By the involuntary powers,
Nights of insult let you pass
Watched by every human love.

LOUIS MacNEICE

1907–1963

FOR X

When clerks and navvies fondle
    Beside canals their wenches,
In rapture or in coma
    The haunches that they handle,

And the orange moon sits idle
　　Above the orchard slanted—
Upon such easy evenings
　　We take our loves for granted.

But when, as now, the creaking
　　Trees on the hills of London
Like bison charge their neighbours
　　In wind that keeps us waking
And in the draught the scalloped
　　Lampshade swings a shadow,
We think of love bound over—
　　The mortgage on the meadow.

And one lies lonely, haunted
　　By limbs he half remembers,
And one, in wedlock, wonders
　　Where is the girl he wanted;
And some sit smoking, flicking
　　The ash away and feeling
For love gone up like vapour
　　Between the floor and ceiling.

But now when winds are curling
　　The trees do you come closer,
Close as an eyelid fasten
　　My body in darkness, darling;
Switch the light off and let me
　　Gather you up and gather
The power of trains advancing
　　Further, advancing further.

WINTER'S COLD

May, and the wall was warm again. For miles
The welcoming air was lighted with smiles
Of homecoming hawthorn. Beat any bush
And a dust of birds flew out: lift a leaf,
There was laughter under. It was a day
For overtones and reveries of thunder.
Everyone walked in a haze, everything
Had a glory of stillness about it: hills
Had their hold-back of story. What shadow
Chilled our talk then? What high word screamed and was gone
Between us? Somewhere in air we heard it,
A stinging thong and rising weal of sound
Like a whoop and whip-round of bees swinging
Above the trees. She shivered, as if to say
'All the hives of our heart have swarmed today.'
Well, we hurriedly tried all sorts of things,
Drenched them in tears of protestation,
Ran everywhere, rooted out old buckets
Of goodwill, rattled odd tin-cans of kinship,
Looked up, of course, the book of usages,
But it was all no good: we could retract
Nothing. Silently
We watched the singing skein of our hopes
Unreel and roll across country
In the calm weather. Has anyone heard
Of them since? Is it, in a sense, only
The winter's cold that holds us together lonely?

AUF DEM WASSER ZU SINGEN

A girl today, dreaming
On her river of time
With April clouds streaming
Through the glass of her eyes,
Laid down her book,
Looked shoreward, and sighed:

'Oh, if print put on flesh
And these words were whispers
From the lips of the poet
In the vase of my face,
Then this punt would be the river
That bore my name for ever
And my legend never fade.

'Then I would understand
What the people of this land
Never understood: his heart
Was torn apart
By a vulture: hence
Fury his address,
And his life disorder.

'I would cling tight to his hand—
The handle of the glass
Where my image would pass
And I saw my face for ever,'
She thought, turning from her lover
Whose need then hung above her.

And he looked up
Across a gulf of rivers
Straight into a face
High above this time and place
And the terrible eyes knew him
And his terrible eyes knew them.

DYLAN THOMAS

1914–1953

ON THE MARRIAGE OF A VIRGIN

Waking alone in a multitude of loves when morning's light
Surprised in the opening of her nightlong eyes
His golden yesterday asleep upon the iris
And this day's sun leapt up the sky out of her thighs
Was miraculous virginity old as loaves and fishes
Though the moment of a miracle is unending lightning
And the shipyards of Galilee's footprints hide a navy of doves.

No longer will the vibrations of the sun desire on
Her deepsea pillow where once she married alone,
Her heart all ears and eyes, lips catching the avalanche
Of the golden ghost who ringed with his streams her mercury bone,
Who under the lids of her windows hoisted his golden luggage,
For a man sleeps where fire leapt down and she learns through his
        arm
That other sun, the jealous coursing of the unrivalled blood.

O MY POOR DARLING

O my poor darling
Legs, arms and round backside
Flanks and thighs hotly eyed
Pawed at and then devoured
Chawed, masticated in
The fiery lion's inside
A sad end for a bride
  O my poor darling

O my poor darling
I thought of Christian martyrs who
Were more disposed than you
To have a great beast spew
Them to eternity
And the later life anew
  O my poor darling

O my poor darling
How could there be a joy
In such power to destroy?
How could such power employ
His glorious rage, to tooth?
How could such teeth annoy
  O my poor darling

O my poor darling
What if the great beast seize
You with its gouty knees?
What if its great lungs wheeze?

What if its cruel gambols were
Age's senilities?
   O my poor darling

   O my poor darling
What is the bridegroom's song?
Lust? to lust in the young
Is to itch in the old man's dung—
Death and age in the genitals
Of youth creep like a worm along
   O my poor darling

   O my poor darling
How cruel that blazing face
How fierce was that grimace
That like an opening was
Yawning and grinning wide
Into a consuming furnace—
   O my poor darling

   O my poor darling
When the saints began to pray
The beast began to play;
When the saints began to play
It lifted up its paw to heaven
And brought it down to slay
   O my poor darling

   O my poor darling
How can an old, aged lion
Liver heart lungs reins stones
Nerves sinew bowels gone
Complete a martyrdom?
What has this bridegroom done?
   O my poor darling—
   O my poor darling

DESCENDING

'I'm going down,' she said, tying her yellow scarf,
While I still watched the dull grey mountain road
Mooch down into the glen and disappear
Round a curve of trees and cottages. Some sudden fear
Made me not reply or make any attempt to start
Yet awhile; I sat on the old sacrificial stone

To which we had climbed all the hot morning together,
Choosing the difficult way, along the dried-up river bed
Choked with dead boulders covered with a fur of spruce leaves.
Not even the sacrifice of our youth—made at noon—redeems
The swinging boughs of our minds, gay with feathers,
Lopped from us now. "I'm going down," she said.

Her teeth were hedges of dense, white sloe-blossom,
Her hair a development of black. Down the afternoon
From the rare peak of youth, too, we are going, to the valley
Of age, lurching and stumbling down its gothic alleys
And grotesque approaches. "I'm going down.' The gossip
Of the wind in her hair will be stopped much too soon.

LINES ON A YOUNG LADY'S PHOTOGRAPH ALBUM

At last you yielded up the album, which,
Once open, sent me distracted. All your ages
Matt and glossy on the thick black pages!
Too much confectionery, too rich:
I choke on such nutritious images.

My swivel eye hungers from pose to pose—
In pigtails, clutching a reluctant cat;
Or furred yourself, a sweet girl-graduate;
Or lifting a heavy-headed rose
Beneath a trellis, or in a trilby hat

(Faintly disturbing, that, in several ways)—
From every side you strike at my control,
Not least through these disquieting chaps who loll
At ease about your earlier days:
Not quite your class, I'd say, dear, on the whole.

But O, photography! as no art is,
Faithful and disappointing! that records
Dull days as dull, and hold-it smiles as frauds,
And will not censor blemishes
Like washing-lines, and Hall's-Distemper boards,

But shows the cat was disinclined, and shades
A chin as doubled when it is, what grace
Your candour thus confers upon her face!
How overwhelmingly persuades
That this is a real girl in a real place,

In every sense empirically true!
Or is it just *the past?* Those flowers, that gate,
These misty parks and motors, lacerate
Simply by being over; you
Contract my heart by looking out of date.

Yes, true; but in the end, surely, we cry
Not only at exclusion, but because
It leaves us free to cry. We know *what was*
Won't call on us to justify
Our grief, however hard we yowl across

The gap from eye to page. So I am left
To mourn (without a chance of consequence)
You, balanced on a bike against a fence;
To wonder if you'd spot the theft
Of this one of you bathing; to condense,

In short, a past that no one now can share,
No matter whose your future; calm and dry,
It holds you like a heaven, and you lie
Unvariably lovely there,
Smaller and clearer as the years go by.

THE ARCHAEOLOGY OF LOVE

You have netted this dawn
From a sea of night
By the moon risen
To find what we forgot,
The palace where
A good prince walked
And a young leopard
Couched on the trees
While suns of oranges
Rose in the orchard.

In less than an hour's
Eternal defeat
By galleys grooving
On the water hate
And oil of peace
In the cruse blazing,
Home became for us
The burning sea
And language a hiss
In the wood of oars.

Through the gorge of fate
We climbed one by one
To a scorpion plain
Dry with poppies
To bury the gold
They gave for our bodies,

And I passed those years
Dumb below pines
To barter freedom
In the land of quince.

By the nets of your grace
I am brought from ash
Of time's shopkeepers
Under the wave
To this island garden
Airy with asphodel,
Your moon raking
My early corn
As the spades ring
On our lost foundation.

I have grown to restore
From dust each room
The earthquakes lower
In a spring of doom,
To piece beyond the fire
The cypress court
With gryphons basking,
Wander in the snow
Of almonds just before
Those petals wasting.

You have taken this night
From sea a vase
Of that dawn in spring,
And the script resolves
To a phrase we love,
You have cut in me a gypsum sky
Happy with harvesters
Fluting the day
Into orange flowers.

You have turned for ever
A generation
Of solitude
Into this field of dawn,
Though doom in waves
Will always march over,
Where I have stood
Dumb below pines
You have brought the dead
To a grove of suns.

NOTES ON SOME OF THE POETS AND POEMS

PHILIP AYRES, 1638–1712, was one of the more interesting and exciting of the minor Carolines whose reputations Saintsbury rescued fifty years ago. He was educated at Westminster and Oxford, was a friend of Dryden, and spent most of his life as tutor in the Drake family at Agmondesham in Bucks. In his *Preface* Ayres shows that he knew his poetry to be, for its time, old-fashioned.

BARNABE BARNES, 1569–1609. Barnes's best poem is his strange and difficult sestina, 'Then first with looks dishevelled and bare', which is too long for inclusion in this anthology.

APHRA BEHN, 1640–1689. The first woman to make a living by her pen. She was a beautiful blue-stocking who lived, as many Restoration beauties lived, no better than she should. She wrote more than a score of plays, several novels, and a good deal of miscellaneous verse and prose. This rather uncharacteristic poem is taken from her novel, *The Lover's Watch, or The Art of Making Love*.

THOMAS BURBIDGE, 1816–1895, was a friend of Clough, with whom he was part-author of *Ambarvalia* in 1849. This was Clough's first book, but Burbidge's *Poems, Longer and Shorter* had appeared in 1838, and in 1851 he published *Hours and Days*.

CATHERINE DYER, fl. 1641. For this, which must surely be one of the most beautiful tombstone epitaphs in England, we are indebted, first to Mr. Hugh Williamson for telling us of its existence, and second to Mr. W. R. Peverly, Rector of Colmworth, for sending us an accurate copy from the Dyer monument in his church.

MICHAEL FIELD, 1846–1914. Michael Field, as was known during their poetry's brief posthumous popularity, was two women—Katherine Bradley 1846–1914, and her niece Edith Cooper 1862–1913. They claimed to have collaborated intimately even in their shortest poems.

IVOR GURNEY, 1890–1937, one of the Georgian poets of the first world war, was shortly after the war confined to a lunatic asylum where he wrote some remarkable poems which were edited by Edmund Blunden in 1954.

THOMAS CAULFIELD IRWIN, 1823–1892, was born in Co. Down, was a classical scholar, a vegetarian, a pacifist, a traveller, and eccentric to the point of mild madness. He published in Dublin and Glasgow many books of verse of varied but often of considerable merit.

THOMAS MOORE, 1779–1852. Tom Moore is of course still faintly remembered for his once famous *Irish Melodies*. The one-time popularity of these obscured and has continued to obscure his excellence in another mode—in those poems which look back to the Restoration, sounding a gay note, at once elegant and dashing, hardly heard in England since Matthew Prior.

MARGARET, DUCHESS OF NEWCASTLE, 1624–1674. Pepys called her 'a mad, conceited, ridiculous woman'. But her epitaph in the north transept of Westminster Abbey accounts her 'a wise, wittie and Learned Lady: a most Virtuous and a loving and careful wife'. Besides poems, she wrote a charming autobiography.

JOHN NICHOLSON, 1790–1843, was one of the peasant or near-peasant prodigies—Bloomfield, Clare, and Ebenezer Elliott were more famous examples—that the early nineteenth century was always on the look-out for. He was the son of an Airedale wool-sorter, and he seemed to be a promising child. But, according to his biographer, 'the pursuits of poetry and an unsettled mind' prevented him from bettering himself, and he remained a journeyman wool-comber. However, it seems to have been drink as much as poetry that kept him back; and it was certainly drink that caused his death by drowning on Good Friday, 13th April 1843. He was survived by his second wife and eight children.

CHARLES, DUKE OF ORLEANS, 1391–1463. The Duke was captured at the battle of Agincourt and kept as a P.O.W. in England until 1460. According to E. K. Chambers and F. Sidgwick, from whose *Early English Lyrics* we have copied it, this poem has no French original, and it may well have been written in English.

COVENTRY PATMORE, 1823–1896. 'The Rosy-Bosom'd Hours' was first published in 1876. The passage beginning 'No sacred bard', and ending, 'your very heart', was, owing to the criticism of some priggish or hypersensitive friend, omitted in all editions of the poem after 1877. 'Amelia' is, unfortunately, too long.

VICTOR PLARR, 1863–1929. This now almost forgotten poet of the 'nineties was a friend of Ernest Dowson, whose Life he wrote in 1914.

THOMAS SPRATT, 1635–1713. Bishop of Rochester, and one of the founders of the Royal Society.

SIR THOMAS WYATT, 1503–1542. 'They flee fro me . . .' is better known in the version printed in Tottell's *Miscellany*. We print the version from the Egerton MS. as used in Professor Tillyard's edition of *The Poetry of Sir Thomas Wyatt*. This MS. is supposed to have been Wyatt's own, and to be partly in his handwriting.

GEORGE MEREDITH, 1828–1909. 'We saw the swallows . . .' Meredith changed the penultimate line of this sonnet, but we prefer the original version. We would, of course, have included 'Love in the Valley' but for its length.

ESTHER JOHNSON, 1681–1728. Swift's Stella and, perhaps, his wife. The question is hardly begged by considering these verses of hers as a love poem—though, as may be suggested elsewhere in this anthology, it is not always easy to be sure when a poem is in fact a love poem. Stella, like many another, rather prolonged her thirty-sixth year.

ANONYMOUS. It is among the anonymous poems that our refusal to consult other anthologies has most probably cost us a few poems that we might have preferred to some of those that we have included. But other poems must have been substitutes, not additions; and we would have been sorry to leave out any of our present choice. 'Constant Penelope . . .' is a paraphrase from Ovid.

EDWARD LEAR, 1812–1888. 'The Courtship of the Yonghy-Bonghy-Bo' is the only not generally considered serious poem that we have included. Lear himself called it a 'nonsense song'; but if all the nonsense elements are subtracted from a poem, you are left with plain prose.

RICHARD MURPHY, 1927–. In 'The Archaeology of Love', a poem which may present superficial difficulties, the poet supposes himself and his Mistress to be standing among the ruins of Knossos. By their love they re-create the town's ancient glories as they look out over the Cretan landscape.

INDEX OF AUTHORS

BARNES, William, 1800–1886
>With you first shown to me
>Since I noo mwore do zee your feäce

BEHN, Aphra, 1640–1689
>By Heaven 'tis false, I am not vain

BELLOC, H., 1870–1953
>How did the party go in Portman Square?

BETJEMAN, John, 1906–1984
>Let us not speak, for the love we bear one another
>In this high pasturage, the Blunden time

BLAKE, William, 1757–1827
>How sweet I roam'd from field to field
>Love seeketh not Itself to please
>O rose thou art sick
>I went to the Garden of Love
>Never seek to tell thy love
>I laid me down upon a bank

BLUNDEN, Edmund, 1896–1974
>Come to me when the swelling wind assails the wood

BLUNT, W. S., 1840–1922
>I see you, Juliet, still with your straw hat
>To-day, all day, I rode upon the down

BRIDGES, Robert, 1844–1930
>I will not let thee go

BRONTË, Emily, 1818–1848
>Cold in the earth, and the deep snow piled above thee!

BROOKE, Rupert, 1887–1915
>Dear! of all happy in the hour, most blest

BROWNING, Robert, 1812–1889
>Never the time and the place
>Dear, had the world in its caprice
>So, the year's done with

BURBIDGE, Thomas, 1816–1895
>She bewitched me

BYRON, Lord, 1788–1832
>So we'll go no more a roving

CAMPBELL, Thomas, 1774–1844
    I'm jilted, forsaken, outwitted

CAMPION, Thomas, 1540–1581
    Thou art not fair for all thy red and white
    Follow your saint, follow with accents sweet
    Follow thy fair sun, unhappy shadow
    Follow, follow
    Rose-cheekt Laura, come
    Thrice toss these oaken ashes in the air
    Shall I come if I swim? wide are the waves, you see
    When thou must home to shades of under ground

CAREW, Thomas, 1598–1639
    Ask me no more where Jove bestows
    When thou, poor excommunicate

CHATTERTON, Thomas, 1752–1770
    Angelles bee wrogte to bee of neidher kynde
    O! synge unto mie roundelaie

CHAUCER, Geoffrey, 1340–1400
    Now welcom somer, with thy sonne softe
    Your yèn two wol slee me sodenly

CHESTERFIELD, Lord, 1694–1773
    Say, lovely Tory, why the Jest

CLARE, John, 1793–1864
    Black absence hides upon the past
    I sleep with thee and wake with thee
    I ne'er was struck before that hour
    It is the evening hour

COLERIDGE, Mary, 1861–1907
    The myrtle bush grew shady

COLLINS, William, 1721–1759
    When Phoebe form'd a wanton smile

CONGREVE, William, 1670–1729
    False though she be to me and Love

CONSTABLE, Henry, 1562–1613
Hope, like the hyaena, coming to be old

CORNFORD, Frances, 1886–1960
I am a lamp, a lamp that is out
My love came back to me

COTTON, Charles, 1630–1687
Alice is tall and upright as a pine
Marg'ret of humbler stature by a head

COWLEY, Abraham, 1618–1667
Underneath this Marble Stone

COWPER, William, 1731–1800
The twentieth year is well nigh past

DAVIES, W. H., 1871–1940
A pretty game, my girl
When I had met my love the twentieth time

DAY LEWIS, Cecil, 1904–1972
I see you, a child

DE LA MARE, Walter, 1873–1956
Who knocks? I, who was beautiful
The far moon maketh lovers wise
The abode of the nightingale is bare

DE TABLEY, Lord, 1835–1895
When we, my love, are gone to dust

DONNE, John, 1572–1631
I wonder by my troth, what thou and I
Who ever comes to shroud me, do not harm
Where, like a pillow on a bed
When by thy scorne, O murdresse I am dead
Blasted with sighs and surrounded with teares
For Godsake hold your tongue, and let me love

DOWSON, Ernest, 1867–1900
Last night, ah yesternight betwixt her lips and mine

DRAYTON, Michael, 1563–1631

    How many paltry foolish painted things
    Since there's no help, come let us kiss and part

DRUMMOND OF HAWTHORNDEN, William, 1585–1649

    My sweet did sweetly sleep
    Though I with strange desire

DRYDEN, John, 1631–1700

    Farwell, ungratfull Traytor

DYER, Catherine, fl. 1641

    My dearest dust, could not thy hasty day

EMPSON, William, 1906–1984

    It is the pain, it is the pain, endures

FIELD, Michael, 1856–1914

    Ah me, if I grew sweet to man

FLATMAN, Thomas, 1637–1688

    How happy a thing were a wedding
    Ye cats that at midnight spit love at each other

FLECKER, J. E., 1884–1915

    Evening falls on the smoky walls

FLETCHER, John, 1579–1625

    Take, oh take those lips away
    My man Thomas

GAY, John, 1685–1722

    The sun was now withdrawn
    O Polly, you might have toy'd and kiss'd
    Were I laid on Greenland's coast
    If the heart of a man is deprest with cares
    I'm like a skiff on the Ocean tost
    She who hath felt a real pain

GRAVES, Robert, 1895–1985

    Presage and caveat not only seem
    Who on your breast pillows his head now

GRIGSON, Geoffrey, 1905–1985

    Cold Oxford unfamiliar now. around

GURNEY, Ivor, 1890–1937
> Out of the blackthorn edges

HABINGTON, William, 1605–1654
> Ye, blushing Virgins! happy are

HARDY, Thomas, 1840–1928
> Hereto I come to view a voiceless ghost
> Woman much missed, how you call to me, call to me
> These people have not heard your name
> She wore a new 'terra-cotta' dress
> At nine in the morning there passed a church

HERBERT, Lord, 1583–1648
> Come hither, womankind and all their worth

HERRICK, Robert, 1591–1674
> Whenas in silks my Julia goes
> Good-morrow to the day so fair
> Thou gav'st me leave to kiss
> Gather ye rosebuds while ye may
> A sweet disorder in the dress

HOOD, Thomas, 1799–1845
> She stood breast high amid the corn

IREMONGER, Valentin, 1918–
> I'm going down, she said, tying her yellow scarf

IRWIN, Thomas Caulfield, 1823–1892
> Why have you risen, to stand with naked feet
> Where in the summer-warm woodlands

JOHNSON, Esther, 1681–1728
> St. Patrick's dean, your country's pride

JONSON, Ben, 1752–1637
> Do but consider this small dust
> Drink to me only with thine eyes

KEATS, John, 1795–1821
> Bright star! would I were steadfast as thou art

KING, Henry, 1592–1669
>Tell me no more how fair she is
>In this small Character is sent

LANDOR, Walter Savage, 1775–1864
>Past ruin'd Ilion Helen lives
>Proud word you never spoke
>Ah what avails the sceptred race
>Mild is the parting year, and sweet
>When Helen first saw wrinkles in her face
>Ye walls! sole witnesses of happy sighs

LANG, Andrew, 1844–1912
>Whether I find thee bright with fair

LARKIN, Philip, 1922–1985
>At last you yielded up the album, which

LAWRENCE, D. H., 1885–1930
>When she rises in the morning

LEAR, Edward, 1812–1888
>On the Coast of Coromandel

LOVELACE, Richard, 1616–1658
>Why should you sweare I am forsworn?
>Tell me not (Sweet) I am unkinde

MACNEICE, Louis, 1907–1963
>When clerks and navvies fondle

MARVELL, Andrew, 1621–1678
>Had we but World enough, and Time
>Ye living Lamps, by whose dear light
>To make a final conquest of all me

MEREDITH, George, 1828–1909
>By this he knew she wept with waking eyes
>Mark where the pressing wind shoots javelin-like
>We saw the swallows gathering in the sky
>Thus piteously Love closed what he begat

MILTON, John, 1608–1674
>   What slender Youth bedew'd with liquid odours
>   Methought I saw my late espoused Saint

MONRO, Harold, 1879–1932
>   Too long outside your door I have shivered

MOORE, Thomas, 1779–1852
>   'Twas a new feeling—something more
>   I've oft been told by learned friars
>   Where is the nymph whose azure eye,
>   Give me, my love, that billing kiss
>   When I loved you I can't but allow

MURPHY, Richard, 1927–
>   You have netted this dawn

NEWCASTLE, Margaret, Duchess of, 1624–1674
>   Love, how thou'rt tired out with rhyme
>   O do not grieve, Dear Heart, nor shed a tear

NICHOLSON, John, 1790–1843
>   The night is calm, the cygnet's down

ORLEANS, Charles, Duke of, 1391–1463
>   My Gostly fader, I me confesse

O'SHAUGHNESSY, A. E. A., 1844–1891
>   Hath any loved you well, down there

OWEN, Wilfred, 1893–1918
>   Red lips are not so red

PATMORE, Coventry, 1823–1896
>   With all my will, but much against my heart
>   A florin to the willing Guard
>   I saw and trembled for the day
>   What measure Fate to him shall mete
>   Within the pale blue haze above
>   An idle poet here and there
>   I saw you take his kiss! 'Tis true

PEELE, George, 1558–1597
>   Whenas the rye reach to the chin

PHILIPS, Ambrose, 1674–1749
    Have ye seen the morning sky

PLARR, Victor, 1863–1929
    Stand not uttering sedately

POPE, Alexander, 1688–1744
    Oh be thou blest with all that Heav'n can send

PRIOR, Matthew, 1664–1744
    The merchant, to secure his treasure
    How old may Phillis be, you ask
    Let others from the town retire

RALEGH, Sir Walter, 1552–1618
    As you came from the holy land

ROCHESTER, John Wilmot, Earl of, 1648–1680
    Absent from thee I languish still
    How blest was the Created State
    All my past Life is mine no more
    'Tis not that I am weary grown

RODGERS, W. R., 1909–
    May, and the wall was warm again. For miles

ROSSETTI, Christina, 1830–1894
    The wind shall lull us yet
    Remember me when I am gone away

ROSSETTI, D. G., 1828–1882
    Piled deep below the screening apple-branch

SACKVILLE, Charles, Earl of Dorset, 1638–1706
    To all you Ladies now at Land

SCOTT, Sir Walter, 1771–1832
    A weary lot is thine, fair maid

SEDLEY, Sir Charles, 1639–1701
    Hears not my Phillis how the birds
    Phillis is my only joy

SHAKESPEARE, William, 1564–1616
>How should I your true love know
>To-morrow is Saint Valentine's day
>When I have seen by time's fell hand defac'd
>Shall I compare thee to a Summer's day?
>How like a winter hath my absence beene
>Let me not to the marriage of true mindes
>When in the chronicle of wasted time
>That time of year thou maist in me behold

SHELLEY, P. B., 1792–1822
>Thou wert the morning star among the living
>A Hater he came and sat by a ditch

SHENSTONE, William, 1714–1763
>Let Sol his annual journeys run

SIDNEY, Sir Philip, 1554–1586
>When to my deadly pleasure
>Ah bed! the field where joy's peace some do see
>With how sad steps, O Moon! thou climb'st the skies

SKELTON, John, 1460–1529
>Merry Margaret
>With margerain gentle

SMART, Christopher, 1722–1771
>Where shall Celia fly for shelter

SPENDER, Stephen, 1909–
>A girl today, dreaming

SPRATT, Thomas, 1635–1713
>Sweet Stream, that dost with equal Pace

STANLEY, Thomas, 1625–1678
>Fool, take up thy shaft again

SUCKLING, Sir John, 1609–1642
>Hast thou seen the Down in the Air
>Why so pale and wan, fond Lover?

WORDSWORTH, William, 1770–1850

    A slumber did my spirit seal
    She dwelt among the untrodden ways

WOTTON, Sir Henry, 1568–1639

    He first deceased; she for a little tried
    You meaner beauties of the night

WYATT, Sir Thomas, 1503–1542

    Madame, withouten many words
    I abide and abide and better abide
    What rage is this? what furour of what kind?
    They flee from me that sometime did me seek
    And wilt thou leave me thus?
    A face that should content me wonderous well

YEATS, W. B., 1865–1939

    Down by the salley gardens my love and I did meet
    Why should I blame her that she filled my days
    Speech after long silence; it is right

INDEX OF FIRST LINES

215

ACKNOWLEDGMENTS

For permission to reprint copyright material, the following acknowledgments are made:

For the poem by W. H. Auden, to the author and Messrs. Faber & Faber Ltd.
>   *Collected Shorter Poems 1930-1944* (Faber).

For poems by Frances Cornford, to the author and The Cresset Press Ltd.
>   *Collected Poems* (Cresset).

For the poem by Cecil Day Lewis, to the author and Messrs. Jonathan Cape Ltd.
>   *Word Over All* (Cape).

For the poem by William Empson, to the author and Messrs. Chatto & Windus Ltd.
>   *Collected Poems* (Chatto & Windus).

For the poem by Geoffrey Grigson, to the author.

For the poem by Valentin Iremonger, to the author.

For the poem by Philip Larkin, to the author and The Marvell Press.
>   *The Less Deceived* (The Marvell Press).

For the poem by Louis MacNeice, to the author and Messrs. Faber & Faber Ltd.
>   *Collected Poems 1925-1948* (Faber).

For the poem by Richard Murphy, to the author and The Dolman Press.
>   *The Archaeology of Love* (The Dolman Press).

For the poem by W. R. Rodgers, to the author and Messrs. Secker & Warburg Ltd.
Europa and the Bull (Secker & Warburg).

For the poem by Stephen Spender, to the author and Messrs. Faber & Faber Ltd.
Collected Poems (Faber).

For the poem by R. S. Thomas, to the author and Messrs. Rupert Hart-Davis Ltd.
A Song at the Year's Turning (Hart-Davis).

For the poem by Wilfred Watson, to the author and Messrs. Faber & Faber Ltd.
Friday's Child (Faber).

For the poem by Robert Bridges, to The Clarendon Press, Oxford.
Shorter Poems (Clarendon Press).

For the poems by W. H. Davies to Mrs. H. M. Davies and Messrs. Jonathan Cape Ltd.
The Collected Poems of W. H. Davies (Cape).

For the poems by Thomas Hardy to the Trustees of the Hardy Estate and Messrs. Macmillan & Co. Ltd.
Collected Poems (Macmillan).

For the poem by Wilfred Owen to Messrs. Chatto & Windus Ltd.
Poems (Chatto & Windus).

For the poem by Dylan Thomas to Messrs. J. M. Dent & Sons Ltd.
Collected Poems 1934-1952 (Dent).

For the poems by Arthur Symons, to Messrs. William Heinemann Ltd.
The Poems of Arthur Symons (Heinemann).

For the poem by Hilaire Belloc, to Messrs. Gerald Duckworth & Co. Ltd and Messrs. A. D. Peters.
Sonnets and Verse (Duckworth).